FISHERMAN
RESOURCES

D1515841

THE ART OF

RESPONDING TO GOD'S VOICE AMID
THE NOISE OF LIFE

SPIRITUAL
LISTENING

ALICE FRYLING

SHAW BOOKS
an imprint of WATERBROOK PRESS

The Art of Spiritual Listening
A Shaw Book
Published by WaterBrook Press
2375 Telstar Drive, Suite 160
Colorado Springs, Colorado 80920
A division of Random House, Inc.

ISBN 0-87788-087-5

Printed in the United States of America
2003—First Edition

10 9 8 7 6 5 4 3 2 1

CONTENTS

Introduction 1

1 Listening for God's Presence 7
  John 4:4-26

2 Listening for God's Love 22
  Mark 5:25-34

3 Listening for God in Scripture 33
  Mark 10:46-52

4 Listening for God in Times of Doubt 45
  John 20:19-31

5 Listening for God in Prayer 55
  Ephesians 3:14-21

6 Listening for God When We Are Busy 67
  Mark 4:35-41

7 Listening for God in Disappointment 78
  Luke 24:13-35

8 Listening for God's Transforming Power 88
  John 5:1-15

Appendix: What Is Christian Spiritual Direction? 99

Notes 103

Leader's Notes 107

Recommended Reading 112

INTRODUCTION

Listening to God is at the heart of the gospel message. God the Father said of Jesus, "This is my Son, whom I love. Listen to him!" (Mark 9:7). To *listen* means not just to hear, but to give heed to, to pay attention to. *Spiritual* listening means paying attention to God. Jesus told his disciples, "Pay attention to how you *listen!*" (Luke 8:18, NRSV, emphasis added). Long before Jesus spoke these words, Moses told the people of God, "Now choose life, so that you and your children may live and that you may love the LORD your God, *listen* to his voice, and hold fast to him" (Deuteronomy 30:19-20, emphasis added).

Jesus said that his followers are like sheep, and he is like a shepherd (John 10:14). He said that sheep listen to the voice of the shepherd and not to a stranger, implying that we will follow him because we know his voice (John 10:3-5). But recognizing the voice of Jesus is a learned art. Unless we know how to distinguish the voice of Jesus from the voices of strangers, we will not be able to respond to Jesus' leading. Part of our spiritual journey is learning to listen to God, to pay attention to the gentle whispers of God's Holy Spirit.

That is what this book is about. It is about listening to God and accompanying others as they listen to God. It is about listening in love. In this book we will look at scriptural passages that show how Jesus interacted with his contemporaries, and from these interactions we will learn how the Holy Spirit might speak to us today. We will consider how we can distinguish between the voice of God and the many other voices that shout out around us. We will learn to listen attentively so we can hear God's quiet voice in the midst of the noise of our lives.

In the process of learning the art of spiritual listening, we will look at the recently rediscovered art of spiritual direction. Because listening to

God is a lifelong learning experience, we need guides and mentors to help us along the way. That is what spiritual direction is about. The term *spiritual direction* is not found in Scripture, but the Bible is full of examples of spiritual direction. The Bible tells stories of "directors" who taught, led, and guided others, as well as stories of "directees" who were mentored and counseled by friends, mature Christians, and church leaders.

Spiritual direction is a term that is once again coming into popular use, although the practice of spiritual direction has been around for centuries. It began when some of the early Christians—Desert Mothers and Fathers—moved out to the desert to get away from the distractions of life in order to listen to God more attentively. Others followed them, wanting to learn for themselves how to listen to God. The Desert Mothers and Fathers then became the first spiritual directors. This kind of mentoring relationship has continued throughout church history (thankfully, no longer in the desert!). Today *spiritual direction* is being reclaimed with its original meaning: two people intentionally looking at one person's life to see how God is leading that person.

When I first heard the term *spiritual direction,* I was decidedly not interested. I assumed (incorrectly) that it described a relationship in which one person *directs* another. I also assumed (this time correctly) that spiritual direction is rooted in the Catholic Church. Since my own tradition is Protestant, I assumed (incorrectly) that spiritual direction was not for me. As I ventured further, almost accidentally, into spiritual direction literature, I found that I had been giving and receiving spiritual direction most of my life, and I never knew it. Discovering the principles of this ancient tradition has deeply enriched my own life and experience of listening to God.

Christian relationships (and the art of spiritual listening) take many forms: friendship, discipleship, mentoring, preaching, and teaching. Spiritual direction is distinct because it is intentional, it focuses specifically on one person's relationship with God, it usually (but not always) happens between an "older" Christian and a "younger" Christian, and it is rooted in an individual's current experience ("Where is God in all of this?") rather than in a program or a preplanned syllabus. A spiritual director is a companion to the one who is journeying deeper into a relationship with God and learning to listen more attentively to the voice of Jesus in daily life. God expresses his love to the traveler through the spiritual director. Listening becomes an expression of that love. Wisdom, direction, and even correction may come through the director, through Scripture, through prayer, or through silence, but ultimately it comes from God. Spiritual direction is intensely personal and touches the depth of our faith experience.

Because spiritual direction is such an effective way to enhance our ability to listen to God, this guide will introduce the elements of spiritual direction as they are seen in Scripture. This is a very gentle introduction to spiritual direction. The appendix at the end of the guide gives additional information for those who would like to know more about the ministry of spiritual direction.

ABOUT THIS GUIDE

At its heart, this book is about being spiritually attentive to what God is doing in our lives. Each chapter has several parts to help focus our attention. First, a Bible study will lead you into an experience of encountering God in Scripture. Interspersed between questions about the Scripture passage, you will find comments about what it means to listen to God in everyday life and about the benefits of having a companion who listens to you as you learn to listen to God. These Bible studies may be done individually or in a group setting, and the interspersed comments can be incorporated into the discussion or read individually before or after the group study.

Following each Bible study are several suggestions for further steps you can take on your own to further develop your ability to listen to God. First, space is provided for you to identify any specific invitation God seemed to be extending to you as you did the study. Then there are suggestions for further personal reflection on the chapter's topic. The section in each chapter called Taking Another Step on the Journey is intended to give you some ideas about things you can do to continue growing in your experience of listening to God in your own life.

You may want to consider working through one chapter each week. You can do the study alone or with friends. Then during the week you can reflect on God's invitation to you from the study, spend some time responding to the suggestion for further reflection, and consider what further steps you would like to take on your own journey. Many of the suggestions for further steps are ones you can do in your own "quiet times." You can write directly in the book or keep a separate journal. Just as spiritual direction is a uniquely personal experience, you will want to use this book in a way that is unique and personal to you.

Finally, each chapter concludes with suggestions of ways you can become a better listener and a more effective spiritual companion to others. You may not see yourself as a spiritual director, but I hope those who use this book will want to become spiritual friends to others in their lives. As you listen in ways suggested in this guide, your friend may not even realize how intentional you are being as a listener. But your friend probably will feel loved and drawn closer to God when he or she is with you. This is a gift you can give even in what may seem like casual conversations.

It is even better if you can listen to a friend in a relationship that is openly intentional. You might say to a friend, "I've really enjoyed hearing about your spiritual growth. Would you like to get together once or twice a month and focus on what God is doing in your life? I'd be glad to listen and dialogue with you if that sounds like a good idea." Another way to move in this direction is to suggest that the two of you get together and take turns—one person primarily listening while the other shares what God is doing in his or her life and then switching roles. We often do this naturally, but I have found that it is very life-giving and helpful to be openly intentional about what is happening. The important thing is to be alert to how God might want to use you to express love and grace in the friendships you have. Begin by asking gentle questions and let the Holy Spirit lead you to deeper questions when your friend is ready.

As you learn the art of spiritual listening in your own life and how to be a spiritual listener for others, remember the Old Testament story of Samuel. When Samuel was a young boy, he heard someone call his name, but he did not recognize that it was God who called. Samuel's mentor, Eli, said to him, "Go and lie down, and if [God] calls you, say, 'Speak, LORD, for your servant is listening'" (1 Samuel 3:9).

May God grace us to be people who say to ourselves and to others, "Listen! God is speaking."

LISTENING FOR GOD'S PRESENCE

JOHN 4:4-26

Several years ago I served on a pastoral search committee. Our job was to find a new pastor for our small church. At first all we had to work with were résumés of people who might qualify for the position. Each résumé attempted to describe on paper who this individual was, listing his or her qualities, abilities, and gifts. As I read through the information, I tried to picture the person each résumé represented. It was not very satisfying. The candidates all sounded similar on paper.

Next we listened to tapes of presentations by some of the people we were considering. Now I was able to engage a little more. Then some members of the committee visited the candidates in their homes and came back with reports. That was even better because we could talk with someone who had actually met the person behind the résumé.

Finally, we met one of the candidates in person. He came to our church. We ate with him. We talked with him. We interacted with him in person. After I met him face to face, the résumé seemed very unimportant. Words on a piece of paper did not come close to the experience of meeting him personally.

My experience with résumés and committee reports parallels our experience of relating to God. From the account of Creation in Genesis and throughout the Old Testament, we read that God communicated with human beings through words and signs, reaching out to them and engaging them in their daily lives. But they could not see God. They could hear about him, but with a few exceptions, they could not relate to him face to face. Then God did an amazing thing. God became a human being so people could see for themselves what he was like. The gospel of John says, "In the beginning was the Word" (John 1:1). Then "the Word became flesh and blood, and moved into the neighborhood. We saw the glory with our own eyes, the one-of-a-kind glory, like Father, like Son, Generous inside and out, true from start to finish" (John 1:14, MSG). In other words, God the Father became Jesus the Son so that human beings could see what God is really like. For those of us who long to have a relationship with God, this is very, very good news.

BREAKING GROUND

(How would you describe your first feelings of God?)

When did you first think about God and wonder what he was like? How have your impressions of God changed over the years?

I thought of Him when I was a young child, and not so much of Him from that point until I was around 50, (1998) It all seemed surreal.

I actually trust Him completely. I may question Him from time to time, but I do know that He has, is, and will work things out for me in His best ways.

✓ What word or words describe who God is to you now?

— Loving, accepting, and forgiving —

LEARNING TO LISTEN

In the four gospel accounts of Jesus' life, we see what God is like. We see how God wants to relate to us. I used to wish that God would speak to me through a burning bush as he did with Moses (Exodus 3:2) or guide me with a pillar of fire as he did the Israelites (Exodus 13:21). I'd even settle for hearing his words through a donkey as when he spoke to Balaam (Numbers 22:28). But I have learned that God's communication with us is even better than those dramatic moments—God is constantly communicating with us through the Holy Spirit, who actually lives within us (Galatians 2:20; 1 Corinthians 6:19). Our job is to learn to discern the whispers of the Spirit in the midst of the noise of life. One of the ways we can do this is to take note of Jesus' interactions with individuals in the Gospels. The way Jesus interacted with his contemporaries suggests the way the Spirit of God wants to interact with us today. Learning to listen to the Spirit is a lifelong process. We learn the art of spiritual listening one day at a time.

Let's look at Jesus' interaction with a woman whom he met at a well in Samaria. In her story, we can see hints of who God is and how he wants to relate to us.

✓ *Indicates further information in Leader's Notes*

Read John 4:4-26.

FIRST LOOKS

1. If this were the opening scene of a movie, what would you see taking place on-screen? What would the set look like? How would Jesus have appeared? What would be the woman's demeanor?

   Jesus would be dressed as a typical man of that time period — resting on a wall around a well. The woman, in old clothes, and weathered drawn skin, would have been lowering a bucket into a well for water as usual. He would have been paying attention to her in a friendly way, but she would have probably tried to avoid looking at him.

2. Summarize the first moments of dialogue between Jesus and the woman.

   He wanted some water after walking so far. He was hot, tired, and thirsty, and he simply asked the woman if she'd give him a drink of water — a simple need.

3. How did the woman respond to Jesus' offer to give her water?

   She wondered why a Jew would ask a Samaritan for something — they looked down on her type of people. Then she said also that He didn't even have a cup to use for the water.

A MEETING AT THE WELL

When this woman left home that morning, I doubt she expected to meet God at the town well! But Jesus, who was God, had a way of showing up in the most ordinary places—in a manger, at parties, out in wheat fields. One of the greatest joys of my own spiritual journey has been learning that every moment of every day has the potential to be a "God moment." My foray into spiritual direction has confirmed that truth. As I meet regularly with my own spiritual director, I often talk about how God is intersecting my daily life. We focus on what God's Spirit is whispering to my spirit.

Unlike the Samaritan woman in this gospel account, I cannot see Jesus in a physical sense. This can be frustrating. But Jesus anticipated our relationship with him today when he talked with his disciples about what it would be like when he would no longer be with them in flesh and blood. What he said is so important to our understanding of spiritual listening for God's presence that we need to look at it in some length. Jesus said,

> I will ask the Father, and he will give you another Counselor to be with you forever—the Spirit of truth. The world cannot accept him, because it neither sees him nor knows him. But you know him, for he lives with you and will be in you. I will not leave you as orphans; I will come to you. (John 14:16-18)

When one of the disciples challenged this, Jesus replied,

> All this I have spoken while still with you. But the Counselor, the Holy Spirit, whom the Father will send in my name, will teach you all things and will remind you of everything I have said to you. (John 14:25-26)

As Jesus continued, his words became even stronger:

> But I tell you the truth: It is for your good that I am going away.
> Unless I go away, the Counselor will not come to you; but if I go, I
> will send him to you.... I have much more to say to you, more than
> you can now bear. But when he, the Spirit of truth, comes, he will
> guide you into all truth. He will not speak on his own; he will speak
> only what he hears, and he will tell you what is yet to come. He will
> bring glory to me by taking from what is mine and making it known
> to you. All that belongs to the Father is mine. That is why I said the
> Spirit will take from what is mine and make it known to you. (John
> 16:7,12-15)

What an amazing statement! Jesus said that, in his physical absence,
he would be present with us in the Spirit. We may not meet Jesus at the
town well (or the local coffee shop) in the same way the Samaritan woman
met Jesus, but God is just as present with us. One of the gifts of a spiritual direction relationship is that it increases our sensitivity to the Spirit's
promptings and makes us more aware of God's presence in our lives. The
Spirit, unlike burning bushes and clouds, will be with us always. And thank
goodness we are not dependent upon talking donkeys!

The Spirit speaks to each of us about different things. I do not see
Jesus as the Samaritan woman did, and she had very different issues in her
life than I have in mine. But I can learn from her experience. She stopped
to pay attention to Jesus. She listened to him. Just as Jesus helped the
Samaritan woman focus on specific areas of her life, so the Holy Spirit
helps me focus on areas in which I need to grow. As I listen for the presence of God in my life, I find that I begin to look at my life differently. As
it was centuries ago, it still is today: People are changed by the presence of
God in their lives.

TAKING IT IN

4. Why do you think Jesus initiated this conversation with the Samaritan woman?

   To establish a loving relationship with the Messiah at that moment and forever.

5. Think about the image of water. What would water have meant to someone living in Samaria at that time? How do the qualities of water compare with the soul's longing for God? Why did Jesus describe the water he would give as "living" water?

   - cleansing, pure, always flowing, satisfies thirst, life sustaining
   - equally the same
   - always available
   meets our spiritual needs

6. Why did Jesus tell the woman to go get her husband? Do you think his question was inconsiderate or considerate? Why or why not? How might the question have helped her?

   - to help her understand a deeper truth
   - considerate and honest
   - true recognition of morality

7. What do you think about the woman's comment in verses 19 and 20? Do you think this was a genuine concern for her or an attempt to change the subject? Explain.

— a genuine concern
— it's all she knew, but it was obvious that Jesus spoke of the future

DIVERSIONS AND BLIND SPOTS

The Samaritan woman did not "get" what Jesus was saying right away. He led her to truth gently and artfully, using questions, theology, and an image. God does the same thing in my own life. The Spirit needs to say things over and over and in different ways before I "get" it.

Sometimes I pull back from the voice of God; I get distracted or even try to sidestep what the Spirit is speaking to me. Learning to discern between my diversions and the Spirit's leading is a continuing challenge. The two places where I get the most help in this are Scripture and community. Scripture helps me because I know the Bible is true. If the promptings of my heart are not in accord with Scripture, then they are not from the Spirit. Community helps me because I find that through dialogue and sharing my life with others, I am more able to discern Truth and Grace. My husband, my daughters, my friends, my pastors, and my spiritual director are all part of the community who walk beside me on my spiritual journey.

Let me give an example of how I have received help in discerning the voice of God in my own life. As I meet with my spiritual director, I often address issues in my life that bring out the themes the Spirit is whispering to me. In other words, when God seems to say similar things over and over, in different ways and in different circumstances, it is good for me to

Just A Note

(light candle)

1- Welcome
2- Prayer
3- Silence - 2 or 3 deep breaths/closed eyes
4- Devotional - from scripture
5- Presence of God in your life this past week - becoming aware of
  — His presence
6- Scripture handouts - 15 minutes alone
                        15 minutes in group
7- Lord's Prayer/Closing

What do you Think ~~you are~~ This
" ~~called~~ ~~to do~~ ?

scripture is saying or what
was it about this scripture that
attracted you? - or drew your
attention to it & more
than the others?

Sallie Evans—

cell: 651 − 1966

Brydon Cooke

cell: 647 − 1746

Dance, Sing, Love

human morals vs. Godly
morals
regarding human ~~xx~~ God-given
Needs —

where is the line of
peace & acceptance felt

(Jesus, Bring Me Closer)

Who are you in Christ?

take note. But because these areas are usually my "blind spots," I need a spiritual director to help me discern the Spirit's themes. One of the themes of God's whispers to me has to do with my propensity to get overextended. I often wrestle with whether to take on new opportunities to serve or minister to others. As I describe these dilemmas to my spiritual director, she helps me discern between those activities I might undertake out of a sense of over-responsibility and false guilt and those I might take on freely out of obedience to God's purposes. The Spirit seems to whisper to me over and over that I need to stop and pray before I plunge into something and that I need to be very attentive to God's invitation to rest. But it would be difficult to see this on my own. Even though God meets with each of us individually, our spiritual journey can never be a solo flight. We need companions along the way.

As we interact with Scripture and our spiritual community in order to listen to God, we may find that the Spirit leads us to use our imaginations, just as Jesus led the woman at the well. He told her that being in God's presence was like having a long drink of water from a spring that would never run dry. Clearly that was a graphic and creative way to communicate spiritual truth to a woman who was used to dragging her water home every day from the town well!

For some people, the idea of using images or our imagination in our relationship with God is a foreign concept, perhaps even a little scary. We have been taught to be objective, even impersonal, in our faith journey. But the truth is that our lives are not objective and impersonal. Dr. David Benner speaks to this in his discussion of reading Scripture meditatively. He writes that coming to know Jesus better—becoming aware of God's presence in our lives—means "lingering over the story long enough to allow yourself to meet Jesus in the account."

It involves daydreaming on what you read.... Imagination necessarily plays a part in this engagement. This makes some people nervous.

Often this is based on a naive assumption that God's revelation of himself can be received in some manner that bypasses the subjectivity of our experience. It cannot. God wants to meet us in our depths, and the imaginative, intuitive and subjective parts of our self must be part of that encounter if it is to be genuine. No one has anything to fear about imagination that is guided by meditation on Scripture and the Spirit of God.[1]

 As we listen for the presence of God in our own lives, and as we help others listen, we may find that the Spirit uses pictures and images to speak to us. When I listen to others as a spiritual director, I often ask them to picture themselves in a specific setting, talking to Jesus about the issue at hand. They may imagine themselves outdoors with Jesus, at a meal with him, sitting beside him on the sofa—whatever picture their imagination gives them. It never ceases to amaze me how clearly we are able to observe God's presence with us when we listen for it in the context of an image or a picture.

Now let's return to Jesus and the woman at the well.

MAKING IT REAL

8. Reread John 4:4-26. See if you can come up with five characteristics of God that are evident in the way Jesus interacted with the woman at the well.

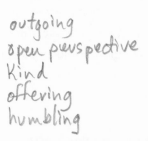

outgoing
open perspective
Kind
offering
humbling

9. At what point in the story do you identify most with the woman? Why?

— why would He want something from me

— He already has everything

10. Verse 24 reads: "God is spirit, and his worshipers must worship in spirit and in truth." How do you personally worship God in spirit? in truth?

— talking and praying to Him throughout the day

— by being totally honest with Him

GOD'S SURPRISES

One of the things I love (but sometimes resist) about noticing the presence of God in my life is that this experience is often full of surprises. Jesus' interaction with the Samaritan woman is full of theological, cultural, and spiritual surprises: a Jew talking with a Samaritan, a man talking with a woman, a promise of water that will quench her thirst forever, Jesus' knowledge of the personal life of this woman, and his understanding of spiritual truths that had been debated for centuries. These surprising parts of the story suggest to me that God desires a relationship with me that is surprisingly radical, unique, and life changing.

Growing in the knowledge of God and in my awareness of Christ's presence in my daily life means letting go of some preconceived ideas. It means holding my ideas loosely and embracing the mystery in Truth. It even means asking questions that may challenge what I was sure I believed. As I become more and more attentive to God's initiative in my life and the Spirit's loving presence with me, I also become more aware that God is not a static being. He does not offer me stale, polluted water. He offers me living water.

Jesus' encounter with the Samaritan woman reminds me that God is with me in all the activities of my day. The Bible teaches that the Spirit of Christ dwells in us (Romans 8:9). This moment-by-moment presence of the Spirit of Jesus makes me very thankful.... *Thank you, Jesus, for meeting us in ordinary places. Thank you for being so creative in the ways you choose to connect with us. Thank you for listening to our questions, for loving us even when our lives are messed up, and for offering us more than we even know to ask for. Teach me, Holy Spirit, to find you at the wells of my life.*

GOD'S INVITATION TO YOU

What new understanding of God's presence in your life is the Spirit inviting you to embrace as you reflect on Jesus' encounter with the Samaritan woman at the well?

- to expect the unexpected at anytime

FOR FURTHER REFLECTION ON LISTENING FOR GOD'S PRESENCE

Spend some time soaking in the reality of God's presence in your own life in light of this verse:

> O God, you are my God,
>   earnestly I seek you;

my soul thirsts for you,
> my body longs for you,
in a dry and weary land
> where there is no water. (Psalm 63:1)

You might want to rewrite the verse in your own words. Or you might picture yourself talking to God in a comfortable setting and telling him about your thirsty soul. Or perhaps you want to think about the spiritual environment where you live and work: How is it dry? How is it satisfying? As you ponder this verse, see how the Spirit of God leads you.

Father, you are my God, and I look everywhere for you. All of me—physically, spiritually, emotionally and mentally—aches and waits for you. I can do nothing without you.

—just trying to be more aware of His presence all day long and to thank Him in all circumstances

TAKING ANOTHER STEP ON THE JOURNEY

If you are not currently in relationship with someone who meets with you at the wells of your life and helps you hear Jesus, consider finding someone who will listen with love and affirmation to your experiences on the spiritual journey. A friend, a spouse, or a pastor who could do this for you may already be in your life. Be intentional about building the kind of relationship where, for an hour or two a month, you are center stage, invited to talk about whatever you are experiencing in your soul.

Asking someone to meet with you to listen in this way may be a new experience for both of you. It may help to read a book together about this kind of relationship. Several books about spiritual direction are listed in the appendix, or you may want to use a more general book about spiritual formation to guide your conversations. One good book for this is *Inner Compass* by Margaret Silf (Chicago: Loyola Press, 1999).

If you cannot think of anyone to meet with you, look at the information in the back of this book about other ways to get in touch with a spiritual director.

THE ART OF LISTENING TO OTHERS

As you grow in the art of listening to God, you may find that others will come to you, asking you to help them grow in similar ways. You, then, become a spiritual companion to them. While you may not feel like an "official spiritual director," you can do much to help others listen to the direction of God in their lives. If someone comes to you and asks you to be a spiritual companion, what can you do to listen in love? Here are a few suggestions:

1. Remember that the emphasis in a relationship where one person listens lovingly to another's spiritual journey is not instruction or problem solving. "The focus of this kind of spiritual direction is the relationship itself between God and the person. The person is helped not so much to understand that relationship better, but to engage in it, to enter into dialogue with God."[2]

2. Remember that in order to listen to another person in this way, we must be humble and respectful. I have found that this means "letting go" on my part. If I want to listen well, with love and awe, I need to let go of my need to be right. I need to let go of many preconceived opinions. I need to let go of my own self-consciousness and insecurities. And I need to let go of the need to appear wise, good, or even spiritual.

3. Remember that in spiritual direction, God is the director. In spiritual listening, whether you are listening as a friend or in a formal spiritual direction relationship, it is to God that we want to direct our listening ears. As you listen, the goal is to help the other listen to the Spirit of God who dwells within. The listener is a vessel of his grace. The conversation in which we are engaged is an ongoing one between God and the other person. It does not begin with us. It does not end with us. In spiritual listening, Jesus himself is the Alpha and the Omega, the beginning and the end.

LISTENING FOR GOD'S LOVE

MARK 5:25-34

"Nearly all wisdom we possess…" wrote John Calvin, "consists of two parts: the knowledge of God and of ourselves."[1] The art of spiritual listening involves looking in two directions at once—looking at ourselves and looking at the God of love. As we listen, we will begin to see ourselves as God sees us.

I have a photograph of my grandson Justin, taken seconds after he was born. He is screaming with rage at having left the womb. My daughter is reaching out for him, wanting to enfold him in her love. He has done nothing to earn her love. In fact, his presence within her body caused nine months of discomfort, and his arrival caused many hours of pain. But I can tell from the picture that all she felt for him at that moment was love.

I keep this picture by my Bible. It reminds me that God loves me right now, as I am. God created me and "brought me out of the womb" (Psalm 22:9). Not only that, but God "knit me together" before I was born (Psalm 139:13). Even more astounding, God *knew* me *before* I was in the womb (Jeremiah 1:5). The picture of my newborn grandson reminds me that God looks at me with loving eyes. He knows me through and through, and he loves me. It is hard for me to believe that. In so many ways I wish I were different, more lovable. But if the Bible is telling me the truth (and I believe it is), then God loves me even more than my daughter loves her newborn son.

BREAKING GROUND

What stories have you heard about your own birth?

— born with severe and contagious skin disease and was placed in isolation for days

When you were growing up, what person in your life seemed to enjoy you the most? What did that person enjoy about you?

— Nan Nan - my grandmother (my mother's mother)

— she loved me unconditionally

A PERSONAL NEED

As children, we are self-centered. As we grow from childhood to maturity, we become more aware of others, we learn to let go of some of our self-ishness, and we learn to look not only to our "own interests, but also to the interests of others" (Philippians 2:4). It is a good thing to develop this kind of maturity. But a problem arises if, in the process, we lose track of ourselves, of our own needs and interests. Some of us work so hard at trying to love others or to be mature or to be "good Christians" that we forget the primary message of the gospel: God loves *us.* In the Gospels we see Jesus encountering men and women just as they are. In this particular study we will look at a woman who came to Jesus with a very private, feminine need. Let's look at her story.

Read Mark 5:25-34.

FIRST LOOKS

1. What was Jesus doing when he met the woman? (You may want to read Mark 5:1-24 to get a sense of what Jesus' day had been like.)

   -He had just come across The lake - where on The other side, he had healed a man from evil spirits.

2. Describe the woman's actions when she saw Jesus.

   -She probably was overwhelmed at just The thought of being near Jesus who heals.

3. What do you think the people in the crowd thought when they saw the woman reach out and touch Jesus?

   - Some may have felt deep empathy for her
   - Some may have felt she was groveling and desperate
   - Some may have thought she was beyond normalicy

A HEALING TOUCH

This woman was desperate. She had had a physical ailment for twelve years, and no one had been able to help her. Her medical condition cut her off from society. (See Leviticus 15:25-30 for the law concerning a woman and chronic bleeding.) She had no more money. She kept getting worse. She must have felt very alone in her illness.

Many of Jesus' encounters with people in the Gospels involved healing experiences. Some of us pull back from the idea of healing because we think it no longer happens or that it happens only under weird, dramatic circumstances. But if we think of healing as *becoming healthy physically, emotionally, and spiritually,* we can begin to relate to the experience Jesus' contemporaries had when they met him.

Today we understand more of the scope of healing than did those who watched Jesus heal this woman. We know there is a mysterious interaction between the body, the mind, and our emotions. We know emotional wounds exacerbate physical needs and that deep healing encompasses both the body and the spirit. Kenneth Bakken, a medical doctor and an ordained pastor, observed:

> Healing involves acknowledging sins and wounds. It involves exploring emotions, memories, and aspects of ourselves that we have kept hidden out of fear.... Healing can be painful, but unlike the suffering that our wounds cause, it is a pain that leads to wholeness and transformation.[2]

As we learn the art of listening to God, we will experience the healing touch of God's Spirit in our lives. The Bible teaches that Christ makes us new creations (2 Corinthians 5:17), transforms our minds (Romans 12:2), and enlightens the eyes of our hearts (Ephesians 1:18). Our experiences of healing may look different in the twenty-first century, but God is still at work in our bodies, minds, and hearts, healing us as Jesus healed this desperate woman. As we return to Jesus' encounter with her, keep in mind the variety of ways God heals us.

TAKING IT IN

4. Why do you think the name of this woman was not given in this report of her encounter with Jesus?

   - she was just an ordinary woman with a big problem

5. If you had been the woman coming to Jesus with a very private problem, what feelings do you think you would have had as you worked your way through the crowd to get to him?

   - can't get to Him fast enough
   - just to touch something from Him
   - desperate to be near His being
   - awe

6. Why do you think Jesus pointed out the woman when she touched his cloak? If you had been the woman, how would you have felt about Jesus' calling attention to you publicly?

   - He notices all types of people
   - overwhelmed, special

7. What do you think Jesus might have been thinking and feeling when the woman touched him as he walked among the crowds?

   - love
   - joy at the prospects of her believing in Him + now having a new life

LONGING TO BE NOTICED

I have never had a physical illness that lasted twelve years, but I can certainly identify with this woman. Sometimes I feel very insignificant, a small part of a very large crowd, clamoring for God's attention. My needs often feel very personal and private. And, like this woman, I sometimes feel as though I have tried everything, and nothing works.

Sometimes my needs are physical, but more often they are emotional, growing out of the natural disposition of my heart and mind. Sometimes I come to Jesus with a sense of brokenness in my spirit. Sometimes I come fatigued and weary. Sometime I am embarrassed by my own needs. I suspect I am not alone in this. It is tempting to ignore these tender places when we think about intimacy with God. They may seem like complications or barriers in the spiritual journey. We may say to ourselves, "You shouldn't be that way. If you would just trust God, you would be different." Often certain aspects of ourselves are—or seem like—handicaps to our spiritual growth and service.

Being aware of ourselves and being honest about who we really are is essential as we listen to God. According to John Calvin, "The knowledge of ourselves not only arouses us to seek God, but also, as it were, leads us by the hand to find him."[3] Learning to listen to God may start with listening to our bodies, to the desires of our hearts, to our preferences of temperament, or to our soul needs. When we allow self-awareness to lead us to Jesus, we find out that he has known all about us from the start. And he loves us, even knowing everything he knows, just as he knew and loved the woman who touched him. When we come to Jesus just as we are, with all of our needs and embarrassing quirks, we can rest assured that he will notice us, accept us, and help us. Sometimes all we need is to be in his presence, noticed and loved. Sometimes we need the healing that comes from his love. Sometimes we do not even know all that we might ask for. According to Scripture, God often gives us much more than we expect (see Ephesians 3:20).

MAKING IT REAL

8. If Jesus saw you in a crowd, what do you think he would notice about you?

— my longingness in My blue eyes

9. When, if ever, have you experienced something similar to what this woman experienced when she felt she was "freed from her suffering" (Mark 5:29)?

— acceptance
— natural high
— wanting to tell others

10. As you think about your own life today, what areas would you most like the Spirit to transform? Without trying to sound religious or pious, tell God your needs. (Someone with the flu, for instance, might pray, *God, I am so sick of being sick. I don't know what else to do. Please help me.* Or someone with a problem at work might pray, *God, I need your help to be able to relate to the person at the next desk. I can't get beyond myself and how angry I feel. Please love that person through me, in spite of me.* Then be silent for a minute or two, just resting in God's presence with your request in mind.)

God, I am tired of not being loved by another human being. Please help me. And if there should be someone at some point, please help to not feel guilty or shameful about my feelings.

11. Jesus said to the woman, "Go in peace" (Mark 5:34). What do you sense Jesus would say to you today in response to your request for help in the preceding question?

"Trust me, Sally, All will be well."

This woman's physical needs propelled her to Jesus. May God give us grace to follow her example, whatever our needs are. May we learn to come to God in prayer, alone as well as in the presence of other people, just as we are.

A SAFE PLACE

A listening relationship, such as a close friendship or a spiritual direction relationship, often provides a safe place where we can express our need for God's help and experience his love and acceptance. It doesn't matter if the need seems big or small, significant or insignificant. If it is important to us, God wants us to bring it to him. Let me give an example of one of my own needs that I often bring to Jesus in the company of a loving listener.

I am an introvert. I get energy from being alone. But I also love people. (As someone said, "It's not that introverts are party poopers; it's that the party poops them!") I often experience the tension of wanting to be with people, to listen to them and love them, but at the same time having a compelling need to be alone. Being an introvert is not a disease that needs to be cured, even though I sometimes feel that way! (I need to remember that extroverts have a different struggle. They are usually energized by being with people. Times of solitude are more difficult for them.) When I come to Jesus for help, I do not ask so much that he will change me or heal me, but that he will give me wisdom and strength to live with the temperament God gave me. Because this is such a persistent problem for me, I find that it is especially helpful to be able to talk about it with someone who understands me and can remind me of God's love and grace.

My needs as an introvert hardly compare to the need of the woman in our study. But, like her, all of us have personal struggles that we want to bring to Jesus. This story reminds me that Jesus notices and cares about me physically, emotionally, and spiritually. His attention to the woman did not stop with her immediate request for healing; he also restored her to spiritual and social community. Since I cannot reach out and literally touch Jesus, I am thankful his Spirit works in those who love me, and that one way I experience God's love is through the care and loving attention of those who listen to me.

God's Invitation to You

As you reflect back on Jesus' encounter with this woman in need, do you sense that God might be inviting you to receive more of Jesus' love in your own life or to extend more love to someone else? Explain.

- all the time and to everyone

FOR FURTHER REFLECTION ON LISTENING
FOR GOD'S LOVE

Spend some time musing or journaling about how you experience the truth of the following verses in your own life: "You created my inmost being; you knit me together in my mother's womb.... I am fearfully and wonderfully made" (Psalm 139:13,14).

Consider these questions: *How does knowing that God made me remind me that he loves me? What difference does it make to me to know that God knew me before I was born? Do I think I am "wonderfully made"?*

I am made the way He wanted me to be. I don't need to know any longer the "why" He made me. I just want to be more aware of listening to and watching for Him. He is my comfort.

TAKING ANOTHER STEP ON THE JOURNEY

Consider praying with a friend about the specific needs of your own soul. It may feel strange asking someone to pray for something that is very deep and very important to you. If you feel uncomfortable sharing and praying about these needs, let God (and your friend) know about your discomfort. It is perfectly okay to feel that way. New experiences often feel strange and uncomfortable. Go ahead, in spite of the strangeness, remembering that God invites us to pray. You may find that the Spirit of God touches you in ways that reflect Jesus' love for the woman in this study.

Here is one way to ask someone to pray for you: Arrange to meet with a friend who knows you and loves you. Ask your friend to sit beside you and—if you both feel comfortable—place a hand on your knee or arm. Ask your friend to represent for you the presence of Jesus' love and to pray silently that God will help you in the area of your life where you feel you most need help right now. (You don't even need to tell your friend your specific need. God knows.) As your friend prays, picture yourself reaching out to Jesus, and picture Jesus looking at you with love. After a time of silent prayer, you may want your friend to say aloud, "Go in peace and be freed from your suffering." (After this you may offer to pray in the same way for your friend.)

THE ART OF LISTENING TO OTHERS

Being a loving listener means setting aside our own agendas, as Jesus did when this woman reached out to him. It means *noticing*; it means focusing on the other person. That person should have your full attention as you listen. Ask questions that will help the other discover the themes of God's whisperings in his or her life right now. Ask about the other's desires, fears, preferences, and needs. By your attitude and demeanor, encourage your friend to be honest and forthcoming. Think about how you might feel if you were in the other person's shoes. What might you need or want that your friend is not mentioning? Ask if that need or desire is present. Ask what your friend would like God to do in light of whatever it is you are talking about. Allow for moments of silence. You do not need to provide correction, answers, or profound insights. Your presence with the other person represents the presence of the Holy Spirit. God is listening. God will provide. God will help. God will heal. Listen quietly, thoughtfully, and with acceptance and love. When we listen in this way, we are standing with another on holy ground.

THREE

LISTENING FOR GOD IN SCRIPTURE

MARK 10:46-52

One day in early March, before the leaves were on the trees, a friend came to visit as I began a long recuperation from surgery. She sat by a window, and I sat in bed facing her as we visited for several hours. While we were talking I let my eyes wander to the scene out the window. I saw birds in the trees that I had never seen there before. Many kinds, many colors. Later that day, after my friend left, I realized that those birds were out there every day. I just wasn't looking.

Reading Scripture can be like that. We can read words without seeing truth. We can become so familiar with the stories that we don't notice their relevance to our lives. We can become so busy that we don't even bother looking. In this study we will explore a way to read Scripture in order to see the truth and grace behind the words. Just as I first noticed the birds in the trees where they were every day, we will learn to look at Scripture and really see the truths God has for us. But first let's look at the experiences with Scripture that we've already had.

BREAKING GROUND

Which word best describes how you feel about the Bible?

Judgmental   Life-giving   Loving   Informational

Boring   Helpful   Interesting

Has your own experience reading the Bible helped you draw closer to God, or has it been a mechanical or even negative experience? Explain.

It gives me hope and reassurance that "all will be well one day" in Christ —

INFORMATION OR TRANSFORMATION?

Before we look at the Scripture passage for this study, we need to step back and look at why and how we read the Bible. In his book *Shaped by the Word,* Robert Mulholland Jr. identifies two ways of reading the Bible: informational and formational. The informational way of reading Scripture is to read for the purpose of gaining new facts, new systems, new ways of living. The formational way is to read Scripture in order to be transformed by God through our reading and our interaction with the Spirit of God. Informational reading is essential to grasp the content of Scripture, but we always need to allow for interplay between the informational and the formational ways of reading. As Mulholland writes,

In information reading we seek to grasp the control, to master the
text.... [I]n formational reading...[you] allow the text to master
you.... [I]nstead of the analytical, critical, judgmental approach of
informational reading, formational reading requires a humble, detached,
willing, loving approach.... A characteristic of informational reading is
the problem-solving mentality. In contrast, a characteristic of formational reading is openness to mystery.[1]

Mulholland says that the purpose of formational reading is "that we might
be transformed from what we are to what God purposes for us to be."[2]

Lectio divina is a way of reading Scripture that invites *transformational*
interaction with God. It is one of several ancient disciplines that is being
rediscovered today, along with spiritual direction, the Daily Examen, and
other well-rooted ways of drawing closer to the heart of God. Lectio divina (divine reading) is such a personal and interactive way of reading Scripture that it is sometimes called prayer. Thelma Hall, a spiritual director and
retreat leader, says "the manner of reading is, more accurately, a 'listening'
and a 'hearing,' attuned to the inspired word and attentive to the Speaker."[3]

Physician and pastor Kenneth Bakken has this to say:

Lectio Divina is a traditional way of cultivating friendship with Christ.
It is a way of listening to the texts of Scripture as if we were in conversation with Christ and he were suggesting the topics of conversation.
This encounter with the Christ and reflection on his word leads
beyond mere acquaintanceship to an attitude of friendship, trust,
and love. Conversation simplifies and gives way to communing, or
as Gregory the Great stated, "resting in God."[4]

My own appreciation for lectio divina was deepened by a conversation I had with my then-college-age daughter. I had occasion to read a

brief short story to her over the phone. My reading, she said, reminded her of the hours we had spent reading together when she was growing up. "It brings back so many memories! Especially the sound of your voice in between the words."

Lectio divina is like that. When we read Scripture lectio divina style, we hear more than we read. Thelma Hall says that "what we hear may be more than the words themselves convey. The Spirit who vivifies them is himself the meaning expressed *through* the words even more than by them, just as a lover may convey volumes in a phrase that would be mere convention when spoken by another."[5] We hear, as it were, the sound of God's voice in between the words.

Let's look in more detail at what is involved in lectio divina, and then try it with a short passage of Scripture.

Lectio divina is usually described in six parts: *silencio, lectio, meditatio, oratio, contemplatio,* and *incarnatio.* (Latin words are almost always used to define these parts. I wonder if they would sound as impressive in English!) *Silencio* is a period of silence before reading the passage. It is a time of letting go of your personal agenda and surrendering to whatever God wants you to experience as you read. *Lectio* is the reading and receiving of the Word of God. It is usually good to read the passage or verse at least once aloud and then once slowly, silently. *Meditatio* is the time of thinking about what the passage says. *Oratio* is responding to the passage by telling God about the feelings you had as you read and thought about the passage. (In meditatio we think with our minds, and in oratio we notice our feelings. Both our hearts and our minds are avenues for God's Spirit to come to us.) Then we move to *contemplatio* when we listen to God, waiting expectantly for the Spirit to whisper to our spirit. This may mean just resting in God's grace and truth. It may mean giving over to God some part of our lives we have been withholding. This time of being with God and Scripture may not even be something we can put into words. It is simply being in God's presence. The last step of lectio divina is *incarnatio,* where we acknowledge any ways that God might be transforming us in our inner being or in our outer activities.[6]

At the heart of lectio divina is the acknowledgment that our relationship with God the Father is primarily through a person—the Word—not words written in a book. Jesus told the disciples, "I have much more to say to you, more than you can now bear. But when he, the Spirit of truth, comes, he will guide you into all truth" (John 16:12-13). Jesus said that the disciples, like us, were not able to hear, all at once, everything they needed to know. The Holy Spirit would come to continue Jesus' teaching. When we read Scripture in a personal, contemplative, open way, we are encountering the Word—Jesus—through the words. This is what lectio divina is all about.

Michael Casey says that lectio divina is "as though God is speaking to us in a new language. We need to sit quietly for a time and let the words flow over us. Soon some sense will begin to emerge from the confusion and new light will illumine the landscape of our hearts."[7]

Now let's experience lectio divina with a short passage of Scripture.

First Looks (Silencio and Lectio)

1. Start with at least two or three minutes of silence. You might repeat the words Mary spoke when she heard she was to be the mother of God: "'Here am I, the servant of the Lord; let it be with me according to your word'" (Luke 1:38, NRSV).
2. Next, slowly read aloud Mark 10:46-52.
3. Read the passage again, silently and carefully.

If you are doing this in a group, work through the following sections (Taking It In and Making It Real) individually and silently. Then you can share your experiences with one another if you choose.

TAKING IT IN (MEDITATIO AND ORATIO)

4. Take several minutes to observe in your mind the scene
   described in Mark 10:46-52. What and whom do you see?
   What do you hear? What do your other senses take in? What
   did the people say to one another?

   *I see all types of people just walking
   slowly on a dusty road. There are people
   begging as well, not just Bartimaeus. I
   see Jesus walking among His disciples.
   I heard voices talking, the sound of donkey's
   hooves pacing the dirt, metal hitting metal
   from the beggars. I smelled food cooking and*

*people talking
about life
and now the
approach of
Jesus coming.*

5. Think about why the people in the passage might have spoken
   as they did. Why do you think Jesus related to the individuals
   in the passage as he did? Let yourself muse on any aspect of this
   scene that grabs your attention.

   *I actually felt as if they weren't paying
   attention to Bartimaeus.*

6. Which person in this story evokes the most emotion in you?
   What feelings do you have about what took place?

   *Bartimaeus —
   His faith in Jesus' healing —*

7. What feelings do you have about Jesus' words to Bartimaeus?

- He wanted to hear from Bartimaeus more
what he wanted - personal exchange

- His command and suredness of healing

READING WITH HOLY GUIDANCE

When you read Scripture for formation rather than just for information, you do not need to respond to all the details of the passage. Ask the Spirit of Jesus to draw you to the places in the passage where God especially wants you to listen. You do not need to work too hard at this. We do not *make* transformation happen. We *receive* transformation. We surrender to it. We give ourselves to what is given to us.

MAKING IT REAL (CONTEMPLATIO AND INCARNATIO)

8. As you "rest with" what you have observed with your mind and with your heart, what stands out to you? Do you sense that God's Spirit is guiding your spirit into some new understanding or experience of his holy presence? Explain.

- to persist in asking for mercy and whatever
I might need, despite how others may
try to distract you

9. Do you sense in your inner being any invitation from God to receive more grace, to embrace truth, or to take action in a particular area of your life? Explain.

yes - knowing and caring for my own
personal needs

EARS TO HEAR

In all of lectio divina, but especially in contemplatio and incarnatio, the experience is very, very personal. But because this is a new experience for some people, I am going to suggest some questions that others have thought about as they have approached this passage with a lectio divina style of reading. Your experience may be entirely different. Do not try to mold your experience to my questions and suggestions. But if you feel tenuous about this way of reading Scripture, other people's experiences might help you identify your own.

Someone might notice that Bartimaeus was sitting by the roadside. That might trigger the personal questions, Where am I *sitting,* emotionally or spiritually, in my life? Is there some place where I am stuck? Is God inviting me to move out of this emotional or spiritual spot? Someone else might observe that Bartimaeus *shouted* to Jesus, and that person might ask, Is there anything I would like to shout to God? Or perhaps someone noticed that people in the crowd spoke *sternly,* and ask, In what ways am I stern with myself? with others? Who is stern with me? How would Jesus respond to my sense of sternness? Or you might notice that the man *threw off his cloak* and ran to Jesus. Is there anything in your life—an activity, a possession, or an attitude—that God is inviting you to throw off? Finally, most of us would do well every day of our lives to ponder the question Jesus asked Bartimaeus, "What do you want me to do for you?" (verse 51). Each day as we come to God in prayer we can think, *What would I like the Spirit of Christ to do for me today?*

This approach to Scripture may seem too loose for some people. We may trust in God, but we may not have much confidence in ourselves to hear what God's Spirit is saying to us. But we do not need to fear making mistakes. We *will* make them. We do not recognize the Spirit's voice correctly all the time. But in spite of this, God continues to work in us and speak to us through Scripture and in our inner being. If we come to him with a spirit of humility and a longing to hear, God will gently inform us, transform us, and lead us in paths of righteousness.

By approaching Scripture in the personal, responsive mode suggested by lectio divina, we are able to listen to God speaking to us personally. We affirm the resurrection truth that the Spirit is as alive and involved with humankind as God has ever been. God longs to communicate love, grace, and truth to us. This is not meant to be difficult. The art of spiritual listening can be as simple as quieting our hearts and minds in God's presence and stopping long enough to be attentive to the words of God in Scripture so that we may live our lives today in communion with Jesus, the Word of God.

GOD'S INVITATION TO YOU

As you reflect on the lectio divina way of reading Scripture, what changes do you think God might be inviting you to make in order to experience the Spirit's presence in the written Word of God?

- being completely honest with Him, so that I can be more in His presence

FOR FURTHER REFLECTION ON LISTENING FOR GOD IN SCRIPTURE

Read through Psalm 119. (It may take two or three sittings.) Note any of the psalmist's descriptions of the Word of God that stand out to you. In what ways have you experienced these truths in your own life? How would you like to experience the truths of Scripture in your life?

-teach me your decrees

-I've experienced many, but I have a long way to go and more to know.

TAKING ANOTHER STEP ON THE JOURNEY

Lectio divina is described many different ways, not always in categories with Latin titles. Sometimes this way of reading Scripture is described simply as the "4 Rs": read, reflect, respond, rest. The following sets of questions offer two other ways of experiencing lectio divina. Whatever set of questions you decide to use, it is most important that you approach lectio divina with a spirit of quiet receptivity. Always begin and end with periods of silence.

Using one of these sets of questions, look at another passage of Scripture. (You might try John 2:1-11 or Psalm 25.)

Set One

1. What word, phrase, or idea stands out to you in this passage?

   free me from my anguish

2. In what ways might the truths around this word, phrase, or idea
apply to your life right now?

— my personal, private lifetime struggle with issues regarding affection

3. What is God's invitation to you in light of this passage?

— to talk with Him and someone else

Set Two

1. What is the main point of this passage?

— to be taught His ways

2. What prayer rises within you as you respond to ponder this
passage?

The Lord's Prayer

3. What promise of God is explicit or implicit in this passage, and
how might that promise affect your life?

— He will take care of me forever

— He makes known His covenant to them

THE ART OF LISTENING TO OTHERS

It is a privilege to share the lectio divina experience with another person. If you are listening to someone talk about his or her current spiritual journey, and a passage of Scripture comes to mind, you can invite your friend to look at it with you. Then you might read the passage aloud one or two times. After reading, allow for several minutes of silence while your friend interacts privately with Scripture and while you pray for God to lead. Then ask your friend what he or she observed, what stood out, or what his or her inner response was to the verses. Listen. Affirm. Try not to interrupt with your own response to the passage. Ask your friend what the Spirit seems to be saying. Again, listen and affirm, but don't interrupt the Spirit. You might end by praying, either silently or aloud, acknowledging to God what you heard. If it seems appropriate, you might ask your friend if you could share your own response to the Scripture when he or she is finished.

FOUR

LISTENING FOR GOD IN TIMES OF DOUBT

JOHN 20:19-31

Gerard Manley Hopkins was an English poet and a Jesuit priest who lived at the end of the nineteenth century. I was drawn to his works while I was in college because he expressed in poetry what I was experiencing in life. One of his poems starts out, "I wake and feel the fell of dark, not day."[1] To some that may sound overly dramatic. But I was in the midst of a long period of depression, and to me, those words brought comfort. Someone out there understood that there were days when I didn't want to get up.

Not everyone experiences the loneliness and discouragement that depression brings. But most of us have had times of deep sadness, of haunting doubt, of debilitating spiritual struggle. St. John of the Cross, a mystic from the sixteenth century, described the times when God seems absent as "the dark night[s] of the soul." He saw these dark times as a gift from God. "No soul will ever grow deep in the spiritual life unless God works passively in that soul by means of the dark night."[2] Philip Yancey writes that the Old Testament is full of "scenes of spiritual failure" when God's people experienced doubt and struggle. "Not only do Job and Moses have it out with God; so do Habakkuk, Jeremiah, and many of the unnamed psalmists. Some psalms merit titles like 'Furious with God,' 'Betrayed by God,' 'Abandoned by God,' 'In despair about God.'"[3]

Yancey goes on to quote Psalm 89: "How long, O LORD? Will you hide yourself forever? How long will your wrath burn like fire?... For what futility you have created all men!" (verses 46-47). As frustrating as our doubts and dark nights might be, we can at least know we are in the company of many saints of God.

BREAKING GROUND

At the times you experience spiritual dis-ease, which word or words best describe your experience?

Discouragement   Loneliness   Frustration   Depression

Doubt   Anger   Fear   Anxiety

- Loneliness-

What do you think "the dark night of the soul" is like?

- being different from people w hom you spend time with routinely

SOUL QUESTIONS

The Bible describes many "dark night" experiences that we could explore. I have chosen the story of Jesus' encounter with Thomas because almost everyone can understand Thomas's doubts. Not everyone experiences depression, but we all, at some time, ask the kinds of questions Thomas asked, whether they are rooted in our intellect, our emotions, or our souls. Let's look at the disciple Thomas.

Read John 20:19-31.

FIRST LOOKS

1. What had Thomas missed by arriving late? What were the other disciples so excited about?

   — Christ appearing
   — He is alive

2. What was Thomas's reaction to their excitement?

   — Doubt but curiosity

3. What, specifically, did Thomas say would quell his doubts?

   — Seeing Christ

LETTING IN THE LIGHT

Most of us can identify with this person who has become known as "Doubting Thomas." Why wouldn't he have questioned the veracity of those who claimed to have seen a dead man now alive? This couldn't be! Like Thomas, I find that much of what I believe contradicts some of my own perceptions of life and runs counter to many of my society's values. My society says that possessions bring happiness. By faith I believe that generosity is of more value than accumulating things. The world tells me I need to look out for myself. My faith tells me I can trust God with my future. People all around me speak and live as though "what you see is what you get." But I want to believe there is much, much more to life than what can be seen and measured. Every day brings new challenges to my choice to live in grace and love. As I look at the tenets of my faith, I am sometimes inclined to say with Thomas, "This couldn't be! I'll believe it when I see it!"

As we grow in our ability to listen to God, we do not "grow out" of doubt. Rather, we learn to listen for God in our doubt. We learn to say with the man who brought his son to Jesus, "I do believe; help me overcome my unbelief!" (Mark 9:24). And what does God say to us when we pray like this? The Holy Spirit may speak to our hearts the same way Jesus answered John the Baptist, who wanted to know if Jesus really was the Messiah. Jesus responded by reminding John to look at the evidence of Jesus' healings and miracles (see Matthew 11:2-6). In some of my deepest struggles with doubt, I have clung to memories of times in the past when I saw God at work in my life.

I am encouraged to remember God's faithfulness to me when I recall what a renowned theologian told me when I asked him to define *faith*. "Faith," he said, "is thinking about God and applying what you know about God to the situation at hand." In times of doubt, then, I recall what I know about God from Scripture and from personal experience, and I remember that even though doubt clouds my vision, this same God is still present with me.

George MacDonald, the well-known Scottish writer of the nineteenth century who deeply influenced the faith and writing of C. S. Lewis, was never afraid to doubt. He wrote, "With all sorts of doubt I am familiar, and the result of them is, has been, and will be, a widening of my heart and soul and mind to greater glories of the truth.... For doubt is the hammer that breaks the windows clouded with human fancies, and lets in the pure light."[4]

Friends can help us let in the light through the window that was broken by doubt. We need to be in relationship with people who are not afraid to hear our fears. We need a listening friend, a pastor, or a spiritual director. Thomas, of course, was able to take his doubts right to Jesus. Let's look at what happened.

Taking It In

4. Why do you think Thomas spoke up so strongly about his need for proof that Jesus was alive?

   — Possibly because he was the only one who wasn't present

5. A week had passed since Jesus had appeared to the other disciples before Thomas actually saw him (verses 19-23). If you had been Thomas, what would you have been thinking during that week? How would you have interacted with the other disciples during that time?

   — I might have felt abandoned by Christ and wondered why He chose that time to appear without me being there

   — I might have stayed away from them because I didn't feel good enough

6. What tone of voice do you think Jesus used during this conversation? What stands out to you about the way Jesus related to Thomas when he saw him?

   — Empathetic tone

   — That he did understand Thomas' doubt, but that He was ready for Thomas to check Him out physically in order to believe

7. What was Thomas's response to Jesus (verse 28)? Why do you think he responded that way?

   — Oh wow! He believed but found it unbelievable!

Speaking to the Heart

Again, I identify with Thomas. So often, the answer to my demanding questions is a "nonanswer." There is no indication that Thomas actually touched Jesus' hands and side. It sounds as if he responded to Jesus with something like "Oh, my goodness! It's true. I do believe!"

It is interesting that Jesus related to Thomas in a different way than he had related to Mary Magdalene several days earlier. After Jesus' burial, Mary went to the tomb, found it empty, and talked to Jesus, thinking he was the gardener. When Jesus called her by name, she recognized him. He told her, "Do not hold on to me, for I have not yet returned to the Father" (John 20:17). He told her to go and tell the disciples what she had seen. To Thomas he said, "Reach out your hand and put it in my side. Stop doubting and believe."

It is easy to think that the Spirit of God says the same thing to each of us. One of the greatest deterrents to artful listening (when we're listening to God as well as to others) is to think that God communicates with each of us the same way every time. Truth is indeed always the same. But Love speaks Truth to each of our hearts in the ways we can hear it best.

Making It Real

✒ 8. Do you identify more with Mary Magdalene in her doubt or with Thomas in his doubt? Explain. (Read John 20:10-18 for the full account of Mary's conversation with Jesus.)

-Thomas (just feels more like me)

9. What helps you the most when you experience spiritual
struggles? Do you need to be alone or with people? Do you
need to study and read or be quiet and muse? In what environment are you most likely to affirm your faith as Thomas did—
"My Lord and my God!"?

*- to center on Jesus, and that He is bigger than
any issue I may have, and that I'm one step
closer to learning more and living more in
Christ*

*- both; alone at first, then talk to a person I care
about deeply*

- nature

10. What is your response to Jesus' comment in verse 29—"Blessed
are those who have not seen and yet have believed"?

- it fits those of us in times post Jesus' life

11. The final verse in our passage about Thomas says that these
incidents were reported in writing so that we might believe
and have life. In what ways is this account of Thomas life-giving
for you?

- I'm reading true events!

LIVING THE QUESTIONS

To believe without seeing is the challenge we face in the midst of doubt.
In my own experience I have discovered that God does not call me to pull

myself up and pretend I believe. The Spirit, rather, seems to invite me to *wait* with my doubt. My Bible dictionary says that one of the words meaning "hope" in the Old Testament can also be translated "wait."[5] As I wait with my doubt, I think I understand what Thomas might have felt during those days before Jesus appeared again to the disciples. I *hope* that what I have heard is true, but I have to *wait* for Jesus to come and speak to me. It is hard to wait.

The German poet Rainer Maria Rilke suggests we need to learn to "live the questions." His words in *Letters to a Young Poet* seem to apply to my experiences with doubt:

> I would like to beg of you, dear friend, as well as I can, to have patience with everything that remains unsolved in your heart. Try to love the *questions themselves,* like locked rooms and like books written in a foreign language. Do not now look for the answers. They cannot now be given to you because you could not live them.... At present you need to *live* the question. Perhaps you will gradually, even without noticing it, find yourself experiencing the answer, some distant day.[6]

I am learning "to live the questions" and to wait with my doubt. But as I do this, I need companions who will be with me. Not everyone listens well to doubt. One of the least helpful things for someone to do for me in my times of doubt is to tell me why I don't need to doubt. One of the most helpful things for a companion to do is to share with me the pain and loneliness that doubt brings and to affirm for me that it will not last forever. Together we wait upon the God who said, "I will turn their mourning into gladness; I will give them comfort and joy instead of sorrow" (Jeremiah 31:13). And we look to the Spirit for the peace and joy that can only come from God.

I am glad Thomas expressed his doubts. And I am especially glad God allowed Thomas's doubts to be recorded in Scripture. God never seems to hide or ignore the faith struggles of the people of God. Jesus welcomes us to come and see for ourselves how his Spirit will help us in the midst of our doubt. God comes into our lives, as Jesus did for Thomas, even if the doors are locked. The Spirit stands in the midst of our daily questions, whatever our experiences, and proclaims, "Peace be with you!"

God's Invitation to You

How do you sense God inviting you to respond to times of doubt in your own life?

✓ - to first be honest with God about my issue

/ - to talk to another human about my issue

< - pray for discernment about this

For Further Reflection on Listening for God in Times of Doubt

Spend some time in prayer, reflecting on Psalm 139:11-12: "If I say, 'Surely the darkness will hide me and the light become night around me,' even the darkness will not be dark to you; the night will shine like the day, for darkness is as light to you."

Taking Another Step on the Journey

Look for a recording of "Holy Darkness" by Daniel L. Schutte. One arrangement I like is sung by John Michael Talbot on his album *Table of Plenty.* In a place of solitude and quiet, listen to this piece of music and let your soul respond to the gift of holy darkness.

THE ART OF LISTENING TO OTHERS

When we listen to people who are in doubt and spiritual pain, we listen *to* them, and we wait *with* them. We wait attentively to see how God will minister to them. As author Tilden Edwards writes,

> Being a spiritual friend is being the physician of a wounded soul. And what does a physician do when someone comes with a bleeding wound? Three things: He or she cleanses the wound, aligns the sundered parts, and gives it rest. That's all. The physician does *not* heal. He or she provides an *environment* for the dominant natural process of healing to take its course. The physician really is midwife rather than healer.[7]

Our presence, our attentiveness, our questions, our responses are all important, but we need to remember that we are primarily observers. "Intense listening is indistinguishable from love, and love heals. This kind of listening means that the people receiving attention are allowed to be the experts on their own pain."[8] We are companions to the one who is on the journey. It is not our journey. But our presence is vital for the one who is walking by faith and not by sight.

By our presence and love for our doubting friend, we are affirming the love and presence of God who spoke through the prophet Jeremiah:

> "I know the plans I have for you," declares the LORD, "plans to prosper you and not to harm you, plans to give you hope and a future. Then you will call upon me and come and pray to me, and I will listen to you. You will seek me and find me when you seek me with all your heart. I will be found by you." (Jeremiah 29:11-14)

This is the God we wait for.

FIVE

LISTENING FOR GOD IN PRAYER

EPHESIANS 3:14-21

When I was a child growing up in the 1950s in suburban Washington, D.C., the arrival of the Good Humor ice cream truck was a neighborhood event. We always heard his bell before we saw the white truck. That gave us time to run inside for the money we needed to buy a frozen treat. (Orange Popsicles were my personal favorite.) I still remember our excitement when we saw him coming. First of all, I would take my life in my hands to step off the curb into the forbidden street. Then I would wave my hand to get him to stop. The driver of the little freezer on wheels would then get out of the truck, come around to take my money, and give me my treat. Oh, the delicious joy of the whole experience!

The problem was that the Good Humor man didn't show up on a regular basis. Monday. Tuesday. Wednesday. Then maybe no ice-cream truck for several days. It broke my heart. So, one summer day I did what children with broken hearts often do. I asked God for help. I prayed that the Good Humor man would come the next day. And he did. God was in heaven, and all was well.

Whether God changed the route of the ice-cream truck so that it came down our street that day, I will never know. But I do know it was the first time I remember praying and seeing results. As my understanding of God and prayer has matured and deepened, I've come to see that my childhood experience of prayer was very, very limited. But it was a beginning.

BREAKING GROUND

When is your first memory of prayer?

— Kneeling beside my bed as a child + praying "Now I lay me down to sleep"

As a child, how did you picture God?

— an old man with a white robe + white beard

A DEEPER UNDERSTANDING

The apostle Paul was one of the great leaders of the early church. We know him primarily as the author of the New Testament letters to the first church groups. But Paul did not start out as we know him. If he had been asked, "As a child, how did you picture God?" I imagine he would have said that he thought God was angry, someone who would kill anyone who broke with religious tradition (see Acts 9:1-2). But after Paul's dramatic conversion on the road to Damascus (Acts 9:3-19), he came to know God as a loving, merciful Father. Paul's prayers for the early church reflect this change in his understanding of who God is. We can learn a lot about prayer from the way Paul prayed for the people at Ephesus.

Read Ephesians 3:14-21.

FIRST LOOKS

1. As you look at Paul's prayer, what words stand out to you?

✐ 2. List the specific things Paul prayed for in verses 16-19.

✐ 3. How did Paul describe God in his benediction (verses 20-21)?

THE TOUCH OF GOD

When we first meet someone, we might shake hands. Some people relate to God like that. Their prayers are like handshakes. They may pray only in table graces or with emergency "foxhole" prayers. The experience of prayer for them is impersonal, occasional, and perhaps formal.

But God desires to touch our lives much more intimately. When I think of God's touch on my soul, I am reminded of the way my husband reached out to take my hand as I awakened from major surgery. My husband's touch communicated intimacy, love, and a celebration of my life.

Paul's prayer reflected his own deep intimacy with God, and he prayed that the people at Ephesus would share in this intimacy. Let's take another look at his prayer.

TAKING IT IN

4. Many people think of prayer as asking God to fix a problem or to meet a need. How is Paul's prayer different from the way we usually pray for people? Which kind of prayer do you prefer? Why?

5. Picture Paul sitting at a table, thinking of the people in the church at Ephesus. One by one they come to his mind. What exactly is he asking God to do in their lives? How would you summarize this in your own words?

6. How would you feel if someone prayed for you like this?

WHERE TO BEGIN

The focus of Paul's prayer is that God would help people experience the fullness of his love. David Benner, spiritual director and author of *Sacred Companions,* has this to say about the love of God:

> God doesn't want me to try to become more loving. He wants me to absorb his love so that it flows out from me.... Only love is capable of genuine transformation. Willpower is inadequate.... Thomas Merton reminds us that the root of Christian love is not the will to love but the faith to believe that one is deeply loved by God.... Embarking on the journey of Christian spiritual transformation is enrolling in the divine school of love. Our primary assignment in this school is not so much study and practice as letting ourselves be deeply loved by our Lord.[1]

This reminder of the essence of the Christian journey not only reflects the love of God that Paul described in his prayer, but it reminds us of the place to begin in our prayer journey. The more we quiet our hearts and embrace the love of God in our lives, the more inclined we will be to pray that others will also experience the Spirit's love.

Paul's prayer is a reminder to me of that truth, and it is also an encouragement to me. In conversations, through phone calls, and by e-mail, I receive requests to pray for specific needs. I think God invites us to be specific in our prayers. But I sometimes wonder if I am praying for the "right" thing. Then I wonder if I am praying "enough." Sometimes prayer feels like a burden. One day, as I was out walking the dog, I expressed this frustration to God. "I can't pray for all of them all of the time!" I cried out to him. Then I sensed the Spirit of God whispering to my spirit, "You don't need to. Pray when you pray, and forget about it the rest of the time." "That's too easy," I said. The Spirit answered in my inner being, "That's grace."

The sense of God whispering to me that day fits with what Richard

Foster says in his book about prayer. Referring to the reminder to "pray always," Foster says that "the literal translation for 'pray always' is 'come to rest.' "[2] Part of prayer, then, is resting in the truth that God hears our prayers and answers us in love. We can pray for our family, our friends, and ourselves, resting in God's love for them and for us. God will do "immeasurably more than all we ask or imagine" (verse 20).

Paul's prayer is also an encouragement to me because I do not understand how prayer works. I do not understand how a created being (me) can talk to the Sovereign Creator (God). Who do I think I am to make suggestions and requests of the triune God who knows all things anyway? Tucked into Paul's prayer for the Ephesians is his request that they would *know* the *unknowable.* He prayed that the Ephesians would "know this love that surpasses knowledge" (verse 19). Paul's words encourage me that I, too, can experience the love of God that surpasses knowledge, and that I can pray that others will experience this love also, even if I do not really *know* how that happens.

Paul's prayer is also an example to me of how to pray. I even borrow Paul's words when I pray. For example, I have a friend who is a graduate student in theology. A growing Christian himself, he is asking the questions, "What is God like?" "How can human beings know God?" and "How do we know what we know?" As I pray for this student, I don't try to remind God of all the things I'd like God to teach him. I pray, instead, that my friend will be strengthened in his "inner being" and that, as he studies and learns, he will continue to be "rooted and established" in God's love (verses 16-17). I can pray with confidence because of Paul's prayer for the Ephesians. It is a special joy to me to be able to pray words directly from Scripture. Then I know I am praying according to the will of God.

Focusing my prayers on Scripture is one of the most life-giving ways I know to pray. It helps me set aside my unanswerable questions and be at peace with my limited maturity and strength. When one of our daughters moved to a distant city, living on her own, I prayed with the words in

Psalm 121, that the Lord would "not let [her] foot slip" (verse 3), that God would "keep [her] from all harm" and "watch over [her]" (verse 7), and that the Lord would "watch over [her] coming and going" (verse 8). I put her name right in the psalm. When I pray Scripture in this way, I do not necessarily know how the truths of the words will work out in life. What I do know is that praying Scripture gives me more confidence and assurance as I pray.

But there is another part of prayer besides our part. In his book *Whole Prayer,* Walter Wangerin suggests this paradigm for our prayers: We speak. God listens. God speaks. We listen.[3]

Speaking and listening are both key components of prayer. I can almost picture Paul praying the words we just read and then stopping to listen. In my mind I imagine Paul thinking about what it would be like as the Ephesians experienced more and more of God's love. As Paul was quiet he may have heard in his own spirit, "This is amazing!" Perhaps it was after a time of silence that Paul began to pray again and said, "Now to him who is able to do immeasurably more than all we ask or imagine, according to his power that is at work within us, to him be glory" (Ephesians 3:20-21).

Of course, we don't know the rhythm of Paul's experience. But I do know that my own prayer life is enriched when I speak and then stop to listen. To listen means first of all being quiet. To stop talking. As we listen for God, we need to remember that God's voice does not sound like our individual voices or the voices around us. When God spoke to the prophet Elijah, he did not speak in the rush of wind or in the drama of an earthquake or in the roar of a fire. Instead, God spoke in a "gentle whisper" (1 Kings 19:12). Another translation says that when God spoke, Elijah heard the sound of "sheer silence" (verse 12, NRSV). When we stop to listen as we pray, we may hear sheer silence. Or we may sense "gentle whispers." The more we practice silence and solitude, and the more we practice listening, the more we will be able to hear the Spirit of God in our lives.

Now let's return to Paul's prayer.

MAKING IT REAL

7. Eugene Peterson translates verse 20 this way: "God can do any-thing, you know—far more than you could ever imagine or guess or request in your wildest dreams! He does it not by push-ing us around but by working within us, his Spirit deeply and gently within us" (MSG). What is your sense of the difference between God "pushing us around" and his working "deeply and gently within us"?

8. Read verses 20 and 21 again. How might the closing benedic-tion of Paul's prayer influence the way you pray for yourself and others?

SURRENDERING TO LOVE

Prayer continues to be a wonderful and frustrating mystery to me. Some-times I wish I still had the innocence of my childhood prayer that the ice cream man would come. Instead, I have complicated prayer with many questions about God and myself. But in spite of all my questions, I con-tinue to pray.

I pray because my heart cries out to God. I pray because my mind knows no better way to be. I pray (according to the popular saying) "as I can, not as I can't." I am encouraged that I am not alone in my questions. Most people ask them. I am encouraged that theologians sometimes give me answers. And I am encouraged that when the answers are confusing, the Spirit comforts me. As Michael Casey says in his book *Toward God,*

> Prayer cannot be measured on a scale of success and failure because it is God's work—and God always succeeds. When we believe we have failed at prayer, it is because we decided what shape our prayer should have, and are now frustrated that there is nothing we can do to implement our ambition. Prayer is nothing more or less than the interior action of the Trinity at the level of being. This we cannot control; we can only reverently submit.[4]

May God give us the grace to surrender to love and to submit to the work of the Spirit in us as we pray in the name of Jesus.

God's Invitation to You

How is God inviting you to stretch and grow in your experience of prayer?

For Further Reflection on Listening for God in Prayer

Spend some time praying, slowly and meditatively, the prayer that Jesus taught us to pray:

> Our Father in heaven, hallowed be your name, your kingdom come, your will be done on earth as it is in heaven. Give us today our daily

bread. Forgive us our debts, as we also have forgiven our debtors. And lead us not into temptation, but deliver us from the evil one. (Matthew 6:9-13)

TAKING ANOTHER STEP ON THE JOURNEY

We may find that the more we try to pray, the more we run into difficulties and questions. Once again, the apostle Paul can encourage us. He wrote to the church in Rome: "The Spirit helps us in our weakness. We do not know what we ought to pray for, but the Spirit himself intercedes for us with groans that words cannot express. And he who searches our hearts knows the mind of the Spirit, because the Spirit intercedes for the saints in accordance with God's will" (Romans 8:26-27). Now that is good news! The Holy Spirit is praying for me and in me even if I feel inadequate in my ability to pray.

One of the ways I have applied this truth in my own life is to experiment with silent prayer. I was introduced to praying in silence by author Thomas Keating. In his books on prayer, he suggests the following guidelines for praying in silence:

1. Choose a word as a symbol of your intention to consent to God's presence and action within. (It could be a word like love, peace, joy, Jesus. Pick a word that comes from your heart.) Keep this word available throughout your prayer time.
2. Sit comfortably. Close your eyes. Now silently introduce your sacred word.
3. Be silent in the presence of God without verbalizing any prayer. If your mind wanders, repeat your sacred word to help you come back to inner silence.
4. Stay in silence for about twenty minutes. (Keating suggests two twenty-minute periods of this kind of prayer each day. This may

seem like a lot to some people. Use his suggestions as they fit your own life.)[5]

It may be hard to quiet your mind. It may feel strange. That's okay. It is important to remember that it may seem as though *nothing* happens during this kind of silent prayer time. The amazing thing is that the fruit of the Spirit will begin to blossom in your life as you practice this discipline. I have a friend who, without my knowledge, was doing this for months. Finally, I said, "There is something different about you. It's wonderful. What's happening?" That's when I discovered she had been practicing this kind of silent prayer, which helped her center her life more in Jesus. If God leads you, praying this way might be another step on your own journey.

THE ART OF LISTENING TO OTHERS

Prayer is at the heart of listening to others. As we listen to others, we are also listening to God. We are praying as we are listening. We are praying that the one we are accompanying on the spiritual journey will be strengthened in the inner being and rooted and established in the love of God.

Prayer is also a frequent topic as we accompany a friend on the spiritual journey. One of the greatest gifts we can give is to invite our friend to talk about his or her prayer life. This is such an intimate topic that we are rarely given the opportunity to explore it at length with someone else.

The following questions are suggested by Jeannette Bakke in her book on spiritual direction, *Holy Invitations.* If you have a close spiritual friendship with someone, you might want to use these questions to guide you into a discussion on prayer. Some of these questions might be good to ask as you listen to someone talk about his or her spiritual journey.

1. What are your prayer practices and how have you chosen these particular ways of prayer?
2. How do your prayer practices include or pay attention to your body, mind, emotions, will, imagination, and memories?
3. Where do you sense an aliveness in prayer?
4. What do you notice about how prayer seems to influence you? others? your life circumstances?
5. What do you think the Holy Spirit might be inviting in your prayer? What makes you think this is God's desire?
6. What are your desires related to your prayer?[6]

SIX

LISTENING FOR GOD WHEN WE ARE BUSY

MARK 4:35-41

In his book *The Contemplative Pastor,* Eugene Peterson tells of the harpooner in Herman Melville's novel *Moby Dick.* Peterson describes the scene on Captain Ahab's whaleboat in which Ahab and his men are using enormous amounts of energy in pursuit of Ahab's nemesis, the great white whale. Melville's book portrays the ever-present conflict between good and evil. But Peterson focuses on the harpooner, the person on the boat who seems to be doing nothing, waiting and watching, poised for the moment when the whale appears. Peterson observes that in our ongoing spiritual conflicts, we need harpooners as well as oarsmen:

> History is a novel of spiritual conflict. In such a world, noise is
> inevitable, and immense energy is expended. But if there is no
> harpooner in the boat, there will be no proper finish to the chase.
> Or if the harpooner is exhausted, having abandoned his assignment
> and become an oarsman, he will not be ready and accurate when it
> is time to throw his javelin.[1]

I would broaden Peterson's observations to say that all of us need at times to stop rowing and be still like the harpooner. We need to have regular times when we wait and watch, intensely and attentively, to see where God is on the horizons of our lives. We need to stand poised for God, listening as well as looking. We need to listen deep within our souls for the gentle, gracious promptings of God to direct us, heal us, help us, and bless us.

One of the greatest handicaps in learning the art of spiritual listening is busyness. The busyness of our lives creates noise and clamor that drown out the whispers of the Spirit. In this study we will look at a time when the disciples almost drowned in the sea. We will compare their experience with ours, when we risk drowning in the waves of life's busyness as agendas and deadlines rise up to overwhelm us.

BREAKING GROUND

On a scale of 1 to 10, where 10 is very, very busy and 1 is calm and peaceful, how would you rate your life right now? How do you feel about the "rating" you gave your life?

Which parts of your life are most apt to generate busyness?

ASLEEP IN THE STORM

Author Dallas Willard, speaking at a conference of graduate students and faculty, startled some of the participants by observing that "Jesus was a very relaxed person." Probably not many at the conference would have used that word to describe Jesus! But Dr. Willard went on to say that, after all, Jesus went to sleep in a boat during a storm. How relaxed was that?!

Let's look at the story of Jesus in that boat.

Read Mark 4:35-41.

FIRST LOOKS

1. Whose idea was it to go out on the lake?

✐ 2. What is a "squall" (verse 37)? Describe what it must have been like to be in the boat at that time.

3. What did the disciples say to Jesus before he calmed the storm? What did they say afterward?

COMMANDING THE WAVES

I have never been in a boat during a bad storm, but I do remember falling into Lake Michigan while I was water-skiing. I remember my panic as the boat sped away and I tried to navigate the very cold water to swim to shore. It is not a happy memory.

It is also not a happy experience for me when I feel overwhelmed by the responsibilities and problems of life. Getting overextended in my commitments is one of the main things in my life that interferes with my ability to listen to the voice of God. When I am overwhelmed by my calendar, I become compulsive about getting things done. I feel inadequate to be all or to do all that I think is expected of me. Usually these expectations creep into my life through bad choices. Sometimes pride prompts them. Sometimes I don't know how I got so overscheduled. One time I added up the number of hours I was committed to activity and responsibilities in a week. Then I added up the number of hours in the week, subtracted time to eat and sleep, and found I had committed to other people ten hours I didn't have!

Because I am so prone to the waves of busyness, I find it helpful to remember Jesus' command to the waves of the sea, "Quiet! Be still!" (verse 39). Let's return to the time when he spoke those words.

Taking It In

4. The disciples ventured out in the boat at Jesus' suggestion. What do you think they thought about his idea when the storm came up and he was asleep in the stern?

5. What would you have said to Jesus in that situation? In light of some of the things in your own life that seem overwhelming, how would you have expressed the disciples' question, "Don't you care if we drown?" (verse 38)?

6. There were other boats out in the lake besides the one Jesus was in (verse 36). What do you imagine was happening in those boats?

FACING THE WAVES

We do indeed live in a world in which we are overwhelmed by global needs, individual responsibilities, and a myriad of unsolvable problems. Whether the waves are attacking our own boat or someone else's, it is tempting to think that we must *do* something to rescue ourselves, as well as send out the lifeboats to rescue others. When we look first to our own resources, we may frantically do more than we should in our attempt to respond to the storm.

Hillary of Tours said that busyness is "a blasphemous anxiety to do God's work for him."[2] Her words hit home. They have hit home in my own heart again and again. When I think I must do something because God cannot manage without my help, or when I think God wants me to stretch beyond my emotional, physical, and spiritual capacity in order to serve the kingdom, then I remember Hillary's words. Pushing beyond my God-given capacity is indeed blasphemy.

Henri Nouwen is another person who wrote about our human need to learn to be attentive to God in the midst of the noise of life.

From all that I said about our worried, over-filled lives, it is clear that we are usually surrounded by so much inner and outer noise that it is hard to truly hear our God when he is speaking to us. We have often become deaf, unable to know when God calls us and unable to understand in

which direction he calls us. Thus our lives have become absurd. In the word *absurd* we find the Latin word *surdus,* which means "deaf."...
When, however, we learn to listen, our lives become obedient lives. The word *obedient* comes from the Latin word *audire,* which means "listening."[3]

Deafness to God, then, is the risk of our busy lives, and obedience to God is the result of listening to the Spirit. But I am still left with the "how to" questions: How do I slow down to listen? When I do, how do I hear? When I hear, how do I obey?

I believe one way to address these questions is to consider the difference between *compunction* and *compulsion.* Compunction is an old-fashioned word that traditionally refers to feelings of guilt, but it can have a more positive meaning. Michael Casey says that "the word *compunctio* points to an experience of being pricked or punctured.... Compunction in this sense is an arousal, an awakening.... The experience may in fact be positive or negative."[4] When we are poised to listen to God, the Spirit may allow us to experience compunction as we pray, read Scripture, or talk with others. Compunction refers to the sense of being directed or pointed by the Spirit to a perspective, an activity, or an invitation from God.

When we speak of compulsions, on the other hand, we are referring to activities and behaviors that we cannot *not* do. Compulsions are attitudes that move us to do things without forethought or direction. The men on Captain Ahab's whaling ship probably fought the waves compulsively, without thinking. The harpooner, however, would have had to intentionally stay still and alert. When I live under the compunction of the Holy Spirit, I live more like the harpooner, intentionally poised to listen and respond to God. When I live like the oarsmen, I fight for all I am worth against the waves of my life.

Now let's return to Jesus and the disciples in their boat.

MAKING IT REAL

7. Picture your life as a boat out in the middle of a lake in a "furious squall" (verse 37). What things in your life seem like waves that may capsize your boat?

8. Why do you think the disciples were so frightened when Jesus did what they wanted? Can you think of a time when answered prayer has frightened you? If so, when?

9. What difference would it make to you right now to know that Jesus is in your boat?

GOD IS IN YOUR BOAT

This is an astounding story. It is almost beyond our imagination to think that Jesus could command the wind and make it die down. It is even more unimaginable to think that Jesus, who was God, was in a fishing boat with these ordinary people out in the middle of the lake. God is in our boat. Now that is *really* astonishing.

The week after my pastor preached about this passage, I went through my days thinking, "God is in my boat! God is in my boat!" This is good news for those of us who frantically fight the waves of busyness and too-full calendars and for others of us whose waves come from the workplace, our families, medical needs, even church.

We cannot stop the squalls from coming, but we can turn to Jesus in the midst of the storm. One of the benefits of being in a spiritual direction relationship is that we have someone already in our lives (in our boats) who can regularly remind us that Jesus is also in the boat. As we describe our storms to a listening companion, our own hearts become quieter. In that quiet space, we may experience the Spirit of Jesus calming the waves in our hearts.

Or it may be that, as we look at the storms in our lives, a friend or spiritual director may suggest that we ask ourselves, Am I in this storm at Jesus' suggestion, or am I here because I ignored the weather report? Jesus is always in our boat. Jesus loves us wherever we are. But it is not God's will that we live our lives on the verge of capsizing every day. In fact, if the waves are caused by too much busyness, as they often are, we would do well to remember the words of Jesus:

Are you tired? Worn out? Burned out on religion? Come to me. Get away with me and you'll recover your life. I'll show you how to take a real rest. Walk with me and work with me—watch how I do it. Learn the unforced rhythms of grace. I won't lay anything heavy or ill-fitting on you. Keep company with me and you'll learn to live freely and lightly. (Matthew 11:28-30, MSG)

This Jesus, who promises rest to those who come to him, is the same Jesus who spoke to the storm at sea. May God give us the grace to listen to his words, "Peace! Be still!"

GOD'S INVITATION TO YOU

As you reflect on Jesus and the disciples in this story, what invitation do you sense God extending to you? Do you have any feelings of compunction from the Spirit that provide guidance in any area of your life? Explain.

FOR FURTHER REFLECTION ON LISTENING FOR GOD WHEN WE ARE BUSY

Set aside some time to sit with the verse "Be still, and know that I am God" (Psalm 46:10). Repeat the verse to yourself, leaving off one word at a time. Be quiet and prayerful as you sit in God's presence. It may help to

set a quiet timer that will help you spend at least one or two minutes with
each phrase.

Be still and know that I am God.
Be still and know that I am.
Be still and know that I.
Be still and know.
Be still.
Be.

TAKING ANOTHER STEP ON THE JOURNEY

Consider committing yourself to the discipline of keeping the Sabbath for
at least three months. One of the Ten Commandments is:

> Remember the Sabbath day by keeping it holy. Six days you shall labor
> and do all your work, but the seventh day is a Sabbath to the LORD
> your God. On it you shall not do any work.... For in six days the
> LORD made the heavens and the earth, the sea, and all that is in them,
> but he rested on the seventh day. Therefore the LORD blessed the Sab-
> bath day and made it holy. (Exodus 20:8-11)

Because we live under grace, this is not so much a "law" as an invitation to freedom. We do not have to work all the time. We are invited to
rest, really rest, one day a week. In fact, I believe that if we follow the Creator's example and obey this commandment, we will actually accomplish
more in six days than we would if we worked seven.

Set aside time to read Marva Dawn's book *Keeping the Sabbath Wholly.*
She writes that as we learn to keep the Sabbath, we learn

> to cease not only from work itself, but also from the need to accom-
> plish and be productive, from the worry and tension that accompany

our modern criterion of efficiency, from our efforts to be in control of our lives as if we were God, from our possessiveness and our enculturation, and, finally, from the humdrum and meaninglessness that result when life is pursued without the Lord at the center of it all.[5]

As we keep the Sabbath, we may find that, for at least one day a week, we can accept Jesus' invitation to join him and sleep in the boat.

THE ART OF LISTENING TO OTHERS

When we listen lovingly and spiritually to others, we have the job of the harpooner. As we listen, the person talking may seem to wander through many different places in his or her life. As harpooner-listeners, one of the things we can do is take note of the themes that we hear, which may reflect some way the Spirit is touching our friend's life. Or we may notice in ourselves a sense of compunction, an attentiveness to something in particular as we listen. Then we can invite our friend to go further. "Can you say more about that? That sounds to me like a place where God might be speaking to you." The gift we give is to listen attentively both to the words of the speaker and the promptings of the Spirit in our own hearts as we hear what is being said.

It is always tempting to drop the harpoon and pick up an oar to start rowing for the one to whom we are listening. But it is much more of a gift to this person if we stay poised and alert so that we can draw his or her attention away from the waves to see God at work in the midst of the storm.

SEVEN

LISTENING FOR GOD IN DISAPPOINTMENT

LUKE 24:13-35

Tears of homesickness ran down my face as I walked away from the dorm, trying to escape the pressures of my freshman year at college. When I came to the retirement community at the edge of town, I sat down on the steps of the building to cry some more. The next thing I knew, one of the residents of the home was sitting down beside me.

"Is everything all right, dear?"

"No," I replied. "Nothing is right…but I guess I'm okay."

We probably talked a little more. I don't remember. But I do know that this woman did not give me any answers. I found no solutions. No fixes. Just an *encounter* with someone who noticed me and loved me. I walked back to the dorm, still crying, but feeling like I could make it through the year.

Life is full of unexpected encounters with other people. Sometimes we notice them. Other times someone graces our lives, and we don't even realize it at the time. When we are in places of struggle, disappointment, or grief, we usually do not want answers. We want compassion, understanding, and acceptance. In short, we want to encounter someone who loves us in our disappointment.

BREAKING GROUND

Describe a time when you were severely disappointed—when something you counted on did not happen or someone you trusted let you down. How did you feel about yourself at that time? What people in your life were helpful to you? What was not helpful?

LOVING LISTENING

Disappointments in life affect our relationships with God. We may "know better," but when we face disappointment, we often feel that God has let us down. How could God allow this to happen? Does God know how upset I am? Does God care? We may even ask, "Is God there at all?"

These questions do not surprise our loving Creator. The author of Proverbs penned the words, "Hope deferred makes the heart sick" (13:12). Sick hearts affect us every bit as much as sick bodies. God knows this. And God hears the cries of our disappointed hearts.

As God listens to our hearts, he often reaches out to us through other people. Sometimes healing encounters are casual, like mine with the lady at the retirement home. Sometimes they are encounters that happen in formal therapy. Sometimes they are spiritually intentional, as in pastoral counseling and spiritual direction. In a variety of ways, we may meet God as others listen to us.

This kind of listening does not seek to solve problems or offer solutions. This kind of listening hears *where we are* in our disappointment and hurt and allows us to be there, loving us in whatever we are experiencing. In spiritual direction, as in other forms of loving listening, the goal is to listen in a way that helps another person encounter Christ on a deep and personal level.

In the Gospels we read that Jesus encountered two of the disciples as they walked together to the village of Emmaus. At the time the disciples were struggling with disappointment and defeat, grieving the death of Jesus, their friend and teacher. When Jesus joined them, they didn't recognize him. Let's look at that encounter.

Read Luke 24:13-35.

First Looks

1. What were the disciples discussing as they walked along the road?

2. Describe the interaction the disciples had with Jesus (verses 17-24). What was Jesus' response to the disciples' description of his death and resurrection (verses 25-27)? If you had been one of the disciples, how do you think you would have felt about Jesus' comments?

3. How did the disciples respond to Jesus (verses 29,32)?

COMPANION ON THE ROAD

Like the disciples, when we struggle with disappointment, we often do not recognize the hand of God in our lives. The disciples felt defeated. This man they met did not even seem to know about the tragic events of the last three days. In fact, he criticized their shortsightedness!

But something drew them to Jesus—enough to invite him home for dinner. I have met people like that, people who seem to know what they are talking about when they talk about Scripture and God. Just as Jesus made the disciples want to hear more, I have met people who have encouraged me to see the Spirit where I thought God was absent and to move toward the heavenly Father even when I was not sure where to look. They have helped me realize that God was with me on my journey.

Often, it is enough to be reminded that God is with us. This can happen verbally or simply by someone's presence. My encounter with the elderly lady on the front steps of the retirement home was enough to remind me that God was noticing me and loving me. The disciples' encounter with Jesus warmed their hearts. But, as he sometimes does with us, God gave them even more than they knew to ask for.

TAKING IT IN

4. When Jesus joined the disciples, they did not recognize him. Why do you think Jesus did not tell them who he was right away?

5. Jesus probably already knew what they were talking about. Why do you think he asked them to tell him about their conversation?

6. What do you think the disciples meant when they said, "Were not our hearts burning within us while he talked with us on the road and opened the Scriptures to us?" (verse 32)? What do you think that experience was like for them?

7. Why do you think it was at the moment when Jesus "broke the bread" that they finally recognized him (verse 35)?

OPEN EYES

Several aspects of the disciples' encounter with Jesus in this passage parallel our own experiences. In times of disappointment and even on regular days, we, too, have had our hearts "burn" with an awareness of God in our lives. It may be in very mundane events that we see the holy. Or it may happen as we read Scripture or other spiritual material. Sometimes something in nature awakens us to the presence of God. Often our encounters with Jesus in other people pull us toward the Father.

But like the disciples, we cannot open our own eyes. Only God can do that. We can only put ourselves in places and relationships where the Spirit is likely to be at work in us. We do not see Jesus with our physical eyes as the disciples did, but, with Paul, we can pray that the eyes of our hearts "may be enlightened" to see Jesus in our lives (Ephesians 1:18). Learning to notice when God opens our eyes leads to a rich experience of intimacy with the Spirit. We are able to see things we missed before. We find that God is engaged with us, walking with us, eating with us, teaching us, and loving us.

MAKING IT REAL

8. When have you struggled with something in life only to find out afterward that God was present in that struggle? What insight did your hindsight give you? What helps you be more aware of God's presence in your life?

9. In spiritual direction, the director often asks the directee to describe the details of a recent experience, as Jesus asked the disciples to talk about their experiences. In what ways does it help you to talk about your own life and your feelings about the events in your life?

10. In verses 28 and 29, Jesus seemed to change his mind. What influenced him? If you could talk with Jesus face to face today, what would you "strongly urge" him to do in your own life?

11. After the disciples recognized Jesus, they hurried back to Jerusalem. How do you think their encounter with Jesus gave them the energy to return all the way to Jerusalem? What energizes you spiritually? When are you most eager to talk with others about your own encounters with God?

The Patience of God

As I reflect on Jesus' post-Resurrection appearances, like this one with the disciples at Emmaus, I am amazed that this man, Jesus, this God-in-the-flesh person had just faced death, conquered it, and was about to return to heaven. Yet he took the time to have private conversations with individuals, to eat with them, to explain Scripture to them. We need to remember that God is just as interested in us today. This is the God who "waits to be gracious to you" (Isaiah 30:18, RSV). The Spirit of God will not force entry into our lives. He waits. He waits for us to notice God, to recognize him, to share our lives with him, to invite him to eat with us. Spirit of Christ, we welcome you!

God's Invitation to You

How do you sense God is inviting you to experience the comfort of the Holy Spirit's presence through your encounters with others?

For Further Reflection on Listening for God in Disappointment

Spend some time in silence, reflecting on Romans 5:3-5:

> We know that suffering produces perseverance; perseverance, character; and character, hope. And hope does not disappoint us, because God

has poured out his love into our hearts by the Holy Spirit, whom he has given us.

Think about how you would define *perseverance, character,* and *hope.* Write this verse in your own words. Then write it again, applying it to a specific situation in your own life.

Spiritual direction question — what does it feel like, to you, to feel the presence of God?

TAKING ANOTHER STEP ON THE JOURNEY

One of the ways to become more aware of God's presence in our lives is to practice the discipline of the Daily Examen. This exercise was first suggested by Ignatius of Loyola, who lived from 1491 to 1556. He spoke about noticing the moments of consolation (joy, peace, and confidence) and the moments of desolation (anxiety, discouragement, and sadness) in our lives.

Ignatius's Daily Examen is reworked in modern language in the little book *Sleeping with Bread* by Dennis, Sheila, and Matthew Linn. The Linns suggest that, at the end of every day, you take a few minutes of quiet. In the silence be aware that God is present with you. Then think of the moments that day when you felt most grateful. And think of the moments for which you felt least grateful. "God's will," the Linns write, "is generally for us to do more of whatever we are most grateful for or whatever gives us most life."[1] The Linns suggest other questions that might help us notice God's presence and guidance in our lives: When did I feel most free? When did I feel least free? When did I feel most able to give and receive love? When did I feel least able to give and receive love?

There are, of course, many ways we can ask the main question: When did I most sense the presence of God in my life today? By doing this examen on a daily basis, alone or with someone close to us, the eyes of our hearts may be opened to see "the hope to which he has called [us], the riches of his glorious inheritance in the saints, and his incomparably great power for us who believe" (Ephesians 1:18-19).

THE ART OF LISTENING TO OTHERS

When people are very disappointed, it seems as though their disappointment fills their souls, crowding out everything else. When we stop to listen in love as someone talks about a disappointment, our listening often creates space within where God meets that person. We can help someone find this soul-space by asking such questions as:

- What were you expecting that was different from what you experienced?
- What words describe how you felt in your disappointment? Did you feel defeated? angry? confused? (You may suggest some possible words, but let your friend pick the ones that fit best or come up with other words.)
- When, if ever, have you experienced this kind of disappointment before?
- What would you like the Spirit to do within you to help you handle your disappointment?

It may seem unproductive to ask questions about circumstances that cannot be changed. But being able to reflect back on a disappointment in the presence of someone who lovingly and prayerfully listens to you almost always leads to more of the Spirit's peace. Our listening, then, bears the fruit of the Spirit in someone else's life. It is a privilege to listen in this way.

EIGHT

LISTENING FOR GOD'S TRANSFORMING POWER

JOHN 5:1-15

Not long ago I signed up for an all-day seminar about helping people grow in their faith through spiritual direction. When I walked into the seminar room, my heart sank. In the middle of the room, the speaker had spread out a large piece of orange cloth with a ropelike something-or-other going down the center. *Oh no!* I thought. *We're going to play some silly game.* But I had committed myself, so I decided I needed to stay and let the scenario play itself out.

Thankfully, the "rope" was not a rope at all, and the intent of the speaker was not to play a game. The rope, she told us, was actually a snakeskin. She had seen the snake shed this particular skin while she was in Colorado. In order to shed the skin, the snake had to get in between two rocks and slowly wiggle itself out of the old skin. What was left, she continued, was a very vulnerable snake with a new skin nowhere near as thick as its old one. She went on to say that what happened to the snake physically is what happens to us spiritually as we grow closer and closer to the Spirit of God. We shed old ways of being, often after we have been between a rock and a hard place. After the shedding we may feel especially weak and vulnerable with our new babylike skin. But the shedding, after all, is the way we grow and is something we can pray for in our spiritual journey.

I came home and looked up *snake* in my encyclopedia. Here is what I read: "The skin-shedding process is called *molting*. For a short time before molting, a snake is less active than usual. The animal's eyes become clouded and then clear again just before it molts. The snake loosens the skin around the mouth and head by rubbing its nose on a rough surface. The snake then crawls out of the old skin, turning it inside out in the process."[1]

How well I identify with that image! When I grow toward God, I find it is often through difficult, tight circumstances in my life. My spiritual eyes often seem clouded as I struggle with some area of transformation in my life. I work hard to "rough up" my thoughts and my feelings so that I can experience whatever the Spirit wants to give me. Sometimes this has felt like turning my thoughts inside out. I almost always feel vulnerable during periods of growth. What if I am wrong? What if my faith is ill-founded? What if I get stuck?

In this study we will look at how we grow and change as Christians. The Greek word *theosis* describes spiritual change, the ways the Holy Spirit works in us to transform us. Theosis is at the heart of our journey. If we do not grow, we remain where we are. If we are not becoming more like Jesus, we are not changing. Our faith is only partly about growing in knowledge through *information*. It is, even more, about growing in our inner beings through *transformation*.

Breaking Ground

List some other images in nature that illustrate the kinds of changes God might want to do in our lives. (*Hint:* Think of trees, seeds, butterflies…)

When has a change in your circumstances facilitated a change in your spiritual life?

Stories of Change

The Bible is full of stories about how God changes people. In every generation of humankind, God has worked in unique ways to transform individuals and communities into something they could not be apart from God's power and grace. The Gospels are full of stories about Jesus' changing, healing, and transforming people. Let's look at one of them.

Read John 5:1-15.

First Looks

1. Describe the scene at the Sheep Gate as it might have looked to Jesus when he arrived.

2. What do you think the man Jesus talked to was like?

3. If you had witnessed this event, how would you have described it to a friend who wasn't there? Talk about what you would have seen and heard, even smelled.

Not a Pretty Scene

If you see this as I do, the scene you described was not a pretty one. The people at the pool were not dressed in their Sunday best. The man Jesus talked to was not reading the Bible or having his quiet time. Jesus intersected this man's life when he was needy, smelly, and helpless. He was *stuck* in his way of life and in his view of life. He wasn't even praying.

I often feel blind, lame, and paralyzed—not in a physical way, but in the circumstances of my life and in my own inability to live out my faith as I would like to. I find myself complaining, to others and to God: "If only so and so would change" or "If only such and such had not happened." If only. If only. (I justify this by saying I am not *complaining*, only *explaining!*) When I direct my "if onlys" toward myself, I cry out as the apostle Paul did, "What I don't understand about myself is that I decide one way, but then I act another, doing things I absolutely despise.... I realize that I don't have what it takes. I can will it, but I can't *do* it.... I've tried everything and nothing helps. I'm at the end of my rope. Is there no one who can do anything for me?" (Romans 7:15,18,24, MSG, emphasis added).

These are the kinds of questions that often come up in spiritual direction. In the safe, affirming environment provided by a loving, listening friend, we may be able to discover for ourselves the same answer Paul found: "Jesus Christ can and does" help us (Romans 7:25, MSG). Let's look again at how Jesus helped the man at the pool.

Taking It In

4. Why do you think Jesus asked the man, "Do you want to get well?" (John 5:6) when the answer seems obvious?

5. If you had been the man, how would you have felt? Read his words aloud in the tone of voice he might have used.

6. How would you have felt when Jesus said, "Pick up your mat and walk" (verse 11)?

7. What do you think of the people who criticized the man for carrying his mat?

✐ 8. The man Jesus healed did not know who Jesus was. Why do you think Jesus didn't tell him right away? What do you make of the fact that Jesus allowed the man to be healed without knowing more about the person who healed him?

GETTING UNSTUCK

This man experienced several of the things many of us experience. Sometimes when we look at ourselves and the circumstances of our lives, we see no hope for real change. To be honest, we may even fear change. We may have a hard time verbalizing what we really want. If we do experience grace and healing in our lives, we may face challenges to our faith, either from within ourselves or from other people. Sometimes, like this man who did not even know Jesus' name, we may wonder if it was God, circumstances, human effort, or something else that caused our growth.

The invalid's experience with Jesus took place out in the open, in public. Most of our growth experiences take place in the privacy of our own souls. This is why it is so important to invite someone we trust into our conversations and interactions with God. Without someone else's perspective, we may wonder if our growth is real. Or we may not appreciate all the implications of change in our lives. Or, worse yet, we may not listen to the promptings of the Spirit that seem to challenge our ways of looking at life.

In the security of a loving friendship or a spiritual direction relationship, we are able to address the places in our lives where we are "stuck." Through dialogue with another person, we are sometimes able to ask ourselves hard questions: Do I really want the Spirit to change me? Am I not receiving what the Spirit wants to give me because I am so set on something else? What do I really want? Is there sin in my life that is hindering God from extending his grace to me?

We do not always need other people to actually verbalize these questions. They are usually inside us already, but we resist them. Some of us resist any line of questioning that seems to come in a challenging, judgmental way. Some of us are so used to hearing the words of our own inner judge that we cannot distinguish the loving but convicting voice of the Spirit. We need someone who will come alongside to help us hear the conviction of the Spirit, which always comes with love and grace. God became man so that we would experience love "full of grace and truth" (John 1:14). Sometimes the Spirit leads us to unpleasant truths about ourselves so that we will receive God's grace. Often we hear God's whispers of grace and truth through the words and encouragement of a spiritual director or someone else who knows us and loves us.

Let's return to Jesus' interaction with the invalid and see how this encounter might parallel some of our own experiences.

MAKING IT REAL

    ✐ 9. Think of an area of your life where you, like this man, feel hopelessly wounded, where change and growth seem impossible. If you were to talk to God about this part of your life, what would you say?

✎ 10. Notice Jesus' words to the man later in the temple, "Stop sinning or something worse may happen to you" (verse 14). Jesus did not teach that all illness is caused by sin, so why do you think Jesus might have said this to the man?

11. When the invalid picked up his mat and carried it on the Sabbath, he was criticized by his peers. In what ways might your own spiritual growth be squelched by the opinions—real or imagined—of others?

THE WHISPERS OF GOD

In this account of Jesus' healing the invalid, we see Jesus doing in the Gospels what he is still doing today through the Spirit: taking initiative in our lives. We are often stuck—in old patterns, in difficult circumstances, in seemingly impossible situations. Sometimes difficulties just happen to us. Sometimes we cause the problems. Almost always we end up bewildered about what to do. Then the Spirit whispers to our spirit, "Do you want to be healed? Take up your mat and walk."

We cannot see the Spirit of God as this man saw Jesus. The Spirit whispers and does not shout. As we mature spiritually, we learn to recognize the voice of the Spirit in our inner being, in circumstances, and through other people. Cultivating the art of spiritual listening means that we become more and more attentive to the whispers of the Spirit around us and within us. As we cultivate and practice the art of listening in our own lives, we find that we are able to use this art to help other people listen for the love of God in their lives. As they listen, they are healed. And one by one we take up our mats and walk.

God's Invitation to You

As you reflect on the Spirit's desire to transform you into the person God created you to be, what do you sense is God's personal invitation to you in this season of your life?

For Further Reflection on Listening for God's Transforming Power

Spend some time reflecting on the reality of transformation in light of Philippians 2:13: "For it is God who works in you to will and to act according to his good purpose."

In what ways do you sense that God is at work *in you?* How does God change your will? your actions? What are some of God's "good purposes" for you?

Taking Another Step on the Journey

The Spirit's work in transforming us is often so gentle, so personal, and so gradual that we do not notice the transformation until after it happens. We need to take time to recognize and respond to God's transforming work. We can learn about how God would like us to respond to the Spirit's work in our own lives from a leper Jesus healed (see Luke 17:11-19). When Jesus healed the ten lepers, he healed them from a distance and sent them off to see a priest. On the way, after they had left Jesus, they realized they were healed, but only one of them returned to say thank you. Following the example of this one grateful person, we would do well to "return" to Jesus now and again to say thank you for the transforming work he has done in our lives.

Take a few minutes to think about where you were, who you were, and what issues you were dealing with five years ago. Make a list of the ways you are spiritually different now from who you were then. In what ways has the Holy Spirit transformed your life? Spend some time thanking God for the Holy Spirit's transforming power in your life. Then listen to Jesus' words to the grateful leper: "Rise and go; your faith has made you well" (Luke 17:19).

listening with gentleness with love with care with compassion

THE ART OF LISTENING TO OTHERS

Sometimes the people we listen to get stuck in unhealthy patterns, as the man at the pool did. How can we listen in ways that will help motivate others to draw closer to God?

Once again, questions are the means of listening in love. With our questions, we let the other person take responsibility for the next step in his or her journey. If someone seems to be stuck, you might ask:

- When have you felt spiritually incapacitated like this before?
- As a child, what motivated you to change? Did you make changes in your life because other people (parents, teachers, friends) urged you to change, or did change for you come mainly from your own inner convictions? What does your own history of personal change tell you about how God might work in your life today?
- How would you most like to experience the Spirit's transforming power in your life right now?
- How do you know if the Spirit is at work in your life?

None of these questions has a "right" answer. And sometimes transformation takes a long, long time. When this happens, our job as listeners may be to just "hold the wounded." We listen, we love, and we wait expectantly for God to work.

WHAT IS CHRISTIAN SPIRITUAL DIRECTION?

Because spiritual direction has a unique place in Christian ministry, it is important to look first at what it is not:

- Spiritual direction is not a relationship in which one person directs another. The Holy Spirit is the real spiritual director. Both people in the spiritual direction relationship look to God and seek direction from him. *looking to God*
- Spiritual direction is not discipleship, where one person guides another through a formal discipleship program. Rather, it is an ongoing relationship in which one person helps another seek God's direction in how to experience love, grace, and guidance as a disciple of Jesus.
- Spiritual direction is not counseling. Although some elements of counseling may be present, the spiritual direction relationship is not primarily therapeutic.
- Spiritual direction is not problem solving, advice giving, or "coaching." It is being a companion to someone as that person seeks God's help and leading in addressing life's daily issues.

According to Dr. David Benner, spiritual direction is "a prayer process in which a person seeking help in cultivating a deeper personal relationship with God meets with another for prayer and conversation that is focused on increasing awareness of God in the midst of life experiences and facilitating surrender to God's will."[1]

This definition of spiritual direction emphasizes the place of prayer, awareness of God, and surrender to his purposes for us. The spiritual director is really the observer-helper for the other person's spiritual growth.

How Can I Find a Spiritual Director?

Spiritual direction is an ancient form of relationship found in many religious traditions. If you are looking for spiritual direction within the context of your Christian faith, it will be important to find a director who supports your faith convictions. It is also important to find someone with whom you feel safe and affirmed. You should feel free to ask about the director's spiritual perspectives before you enter into a spiritual direction relationship.

The ability to listen with love, wisdom, and insight is the gift given to spiritual directors. Some people have this gift and express it in their everyday relationships but do not consider themselves spiritual directors. It may be that you have a friend with this gift who will be your "sacred companion." Other people who have this gift of listening choose to use it specifically within the context of formal spiritual direction. They may have completed a training program to equip them to use their gifts more fully. If you choose to go to someone you do not know personally, you can ask about his or her training to learn something about his or her perspective on spiritual direction.   *Sacred guide*

One of the best places to begin looking for a spiritual director is to ask a friend who is already seeing someone for spiritual direction. This is a good starting point for learning about the network of spiritual directors in your area. You might also want to check with your church or denomination. Some denominations have departments of spiritual formation and may be able to give you the names of local spiritual directors within the denomination. You could also contact Spiritual Directors International and ask them for the name of someone near you who offers spiritual direction. (Spiritual Directors International, P.O. Box 25469, Seattle, WA 98125. Phone: 425-455-1565; e-mail: office@sdiworld.org; Web site: www.sdiworld.org.)

Spiritual direction is an intimate relationship. You will probably want to meet with your potential spiritual director at least once to see if you sense a spiritual and relational fit. If you do, you might set up two or three appointments and then take time to evaluate and see if things are working.

People usually see their spiritual directors once or twice a month for at least an hour at a time. Some spiritual directors have a set fee, some ask for whatever financial reimbursement you would like to give, and some offer spiritual direction without charge. Spiritual direction conversations should take place in a quiet setting. Some directors meet people in their homes or at local churches, and some even offer direction by phone or e-mail. Feel free to ask any logistical questions you have.

As you think about starting out on a journey into spiritual direction, begin by asking the Holy Spirit to lead you to someone who will love you with God's love. Talk to friends who are in spiritual direction. Read books about it. Keep looking until you sense that you are where God will meet you personally in your daily experiences.

How Do I Become a Spiritual Director?

Spiritual direction is a gift that is usually recognized in hindsight. The person considering becoming a spiritual director has already noticed that people have come to him or her asking for help in spiritual growth. In my own life, training in spiritual direction became a tool to help me improve what I had been doing for years, informally. Since I completed my training, I have had a deepening sense that this is a gift and a call from God that could be given only by the Holy Spirit. To listen to others in this way is, indeed, a holy calling.

Many programs are available for those considering training in spiritual direction. Most of these training programs offer certification in spiritual direction, although the word *certification* is a misnomer. There is no standard certification for spiritual direction since it is considered to be a gift from God. But there is a remarkable consistency in the training that is offered. Usually this is a two-year program, including units on prayer, theology, human development, spiritual formation, and spiritual direction. These programs are sometimes offered by extension as well as on-site. They usually include some residential retreat times. Some programs are unique to their denominations or to specific Catholic orders. Some seem to be more academic, while others are more relational. Some are clearly Christian, while others intentionally include many religious traditions.

The best way to find a program that suits your own sense of calling is to talk to people who have been through one of the programs. You can write to any program center and ask for information. Many spiritual direction programs have Web sites. Spiritual Directors International may be able to help you find out about programs in your area.

Don't try to talk yourself into becoming a spiritual director as though this is something you "should" do. Spiritual direction is a calling from God, not primarily a professional undertaking. Each individual and each program is unique. Look for the custom-made purpose of God for your life. If God leads you into spiritual direction, you will find it life-giving, life changing, and Spirit-filled.

NOTES

STUDY 1: LISTENING FOR GOD'S PRESENCE

1. David G. Benner, *Sacred Companions* (Downers Grove, Ill.: InterVarsity, 2002), 111.
2. William A. Barry and William J. Connolly, *The Practice of Spiritual Direction* (San Francisco: HarperSanFrancisco, 1986), 6-7.

STUDY 2: LISTENING FOR GOD'S LOVE

1. John Calvin, *Institutes of the Christian Religion* (Grand Rapids: Eerdmans, 1995), quoted in Carolyn Nystrom, *John Calvin: Sovereign Hope* (Downers Grove, Ill.: InterVarsity, 2002), 13.
2. Kenneth Bakken, *The Journey into God* (Minneapolis: Augsburg, 2000), 152-3.
3. Calvin, quoted in Nystrom, *John Calvin,* 14.

STUDY 3: LISTENING FOR GOD IN SCRIPTURE

1. M. Robert Mulholland Jr., *Shaped by the Word* (Nashville: The Upper Room, 1985), 54-7.
2. Mulholland, *Shaped by the Word,* 155.
3. Thelma Hall, *Too Deep for Words* (New York: Paulist, 1988), 36.
4. Bakken, *The Journey into God,* 25.
5. Hall, *Too Deep for Words,* 37.
6. A more complete description of the lectio process can be found in *Invitation to a Journey* by M. Robert Mulholland Jr. (Downers Grove, Ill.: InterVarsity, 1993).

7. Michael Casey, *Sacred Reading* (Liguori, Mo.: Liguori Publications, 1995), 89.

STUDY 4: LISTENING FOR GOD IN TIMES OF DOUBT

1. Gerard Manley Hopkins, "I wake and feel the fell of dark," quoted in *Chief Modern Poets of England and America*, eds. Sanders, Nelson, and Rosenthal (New York: Macmillan, 1957), 1-67.
2. St. John of the Cross, *The Dark Night of the Soul* (New York: Doubleday, Image Books, 1959), quoted in Richard Foster, *Devotional Classics* (San Francisco: HarperSanFrancisco, 1993), 36.
3. Philip Yancey, *The Bible Jesus Read* (Grand Rapids: Zondervan, 1999), 121.
4. Michael R. Phillips, *George MacDonald: Scotland's Beloved Storyteller* (Minneapolis: Bethany, 1987), 311.
5. Lawrence O. Richards, *Expository Dictionary of Bible Words* (Grand Rapids: Zondervan, 1985), 343.
6. Rainer Maria Rilke, *Letters to a Young Poet* (Novato, Calif.: New World Library, 2000), 35.
7. Tilden Edwards, *Spiritual Friend* (New York: Paulist, 1980), 125.
8. Ken Blue, *Authority to Heal* (Downers Grove, Ill.: InterVarsity, 1987), 128.

STUDY 5: LISTENING FOR GOD IN PRAYER

1. Benner, *Sacred Companions*, 34.
2. Richard Foster, *Prayer* (San Francisco: HarperSanFrancisco, 1992), 96.

3. Walter Wangerin, Jr., *Whole Prayer* (Grand Rapids: Zondervan, 1998). This schema is introduced on page 29.

4. Michael Casey, *Toward God* (Liguori, Mo.: Liguori/Triumph, 1995), 35.

5. These steps are taken from Keating's books on prayer. You can find out more about this kind of prayer from his books *Open Mind, Open Heart* (New York: Continuum, 1995) and *Intimacy with God* (New York: Crossroad, 1994). Or you can go to the Web site www.contemplativeoutreach.org.

6. Jeannette A. Bakke, *Holy Invitations* (Grand Rapids: Baker, 2000), 210.

STUDY 6: LISTENING FOR GOD WHEN WE ARE BUSY

1. Eugene Peterson, *The Contemplative Pastor* (Grand Rapids: Eerdmans, 1989), 24.

2. Hillary of Tours, quoted in Peterson, *The Contemplative Pastor,* 18.

3. Henri J. M. Nouwen, *Making All Things New* (San Francisco: HarperSanFrancisco, 1981), 67.

4. Casey, *Toward God,* 43.

5. Marva Dawn, *Keeping the Sabbath Wholly,* (Grand Rapids: Eerdmans, 1989), 3.

STUDY 7: LISTENING FOR GOD IN DISAPPOINTMENT

1. Dennis Linn, Sheila Fabricant Linn, and Matthew Linn, *Sleeping with Bread* (Mahwah, N.J.: Paulist, 1995), 4.

Study 8: Listening for God's Transforming Power

1. *The World Book Encyclopedia,* 1989, s.v. "snake."

Appendix: What Is Christian Spiritual Direction?

1. Benner, *Sacred Companions,* 94.

LEADER'S NOTES

STUDY 1: LISTENING FOR GOD'S PRESENCE

Breaking Ground. You might want to suggest some possibilities—friend, teacher, mother, father, police officer, shepherd, drill sergeant, lover.

Question 6. We cannot, of course, know precisely what motivated Jesus' comment about the woman's husband, but there is no indication she felt defensive or manipulated. Jesus simply said to her what she herself acknowledged was true. Perhaps Jesus' question was a kind way to help the woman express the truth about herself. Sometimes saying the truth about ourselves, even when it is not good, opens us to hearing more from Jesus.

STUDY 2: LISTENING FOR GOD'S LOVE

Question 3. According to Bible scholar Donald English, this woman's illness would have made her "unclean" in Jewish tradition, which "may account in part for her furtive approach." English adds, "The touching of the garment was related to a common belief at the time that the clothing carried the power of the person" (Donald English, *The Message of Mark*, Downers Grove, Ill.: InterVarsity, 1992, p. 115).

Question 6. Even though she was afraid, the woman might have experienced several benefits from Jesus' public acknowledgment. Her peers would now know that she was healed and therefore ceremonially clean. She would have heard from Jesus that her faith brought about her healing. And she would have heard Jesus giving her peace.

Question 10. One way to discover areas in your life that the Spirit might want to transform is to notice the deep desires of your heart. Read Psalm 37:4. Our longings often indicate places where God is at work in us.

STUDY 3: LISTENING FOR GOD IN SCRIPTURE

Question 1. If you are doing this study in a group, allow enough time of silence for each member of the group to come personally before God.

Question 2. In a group, ask one person to read the passage aloud.

Question 3. Allow enough time for everyone to read silently at their own pace. You might ask people to look up when they are done, so no one will feel rushed and you will know when to move on.

Question 8. After you spend time with your thoughts and feelings about the passage, sit quietly in the presence of God. It may seem strange to no longer concentrate on your thoughts or feelings. Just be with God and Scripture. This is a difficult process to describe, but Gregory the Great's words "resting in God" come close to describing this part of lectio divina.

STUDY 4: LISTENING FOR GOD IN TIMES OF DOUBT

Question 6. If you are in a group, it might be interesting to have two people read the dialogue between Jesus and Thomas. Read it two or three times, using different tones and different interpretations.

Question 8. It is interesting to note that while Peter and the other disciple rushed away from the empty tomb, Mary stayed. Because she listened to her grief and doubt and stayed at the tomb, in tears, she became the first person to see the resurrected Jesus. Our fears, our doubts, and our tears may actually lead us into the presence of Jesus.

STUDY 5: LISTENING FOR GOD IN PRAYER

Questions 2 and 3. Try to answer these questions using your own words rather than just repeating what Paul said.

Question 4. Paul's requests apply to all of life, not just one or two specific needs. His prayer is for changes within us rather than in our circumstances.

Question 8. Again, it might help to restate Paul's prayer in your own words.

STUDY 6: LISTENING FOR GOD WHEN WE ARE BUSY

Question 2. Other translations of Mark 4:37 read "a great storm of wind" (RSV) and "a furious storm of wind [of hurricane proportions]" (AMP).

Question 7. Not all waves in our lives come from busyness. Any crisis or struggle may feel overwhelming. If you are doing this study in a group, allow people to identify their own waves.

STUDY 7: LISTENING FOR GOD IN DISAPPOINTMENT

Question 4. This is not the only post-Resurrection occasion when Jesus was not recognized. See John 20:14 and John 21:4.

Question 7. Professor of New Testament Darrell Bock writes, "It is in the intimacy of fellowship that Jesus is recognized. This setting is no mistake.... Many of the resurrection appearances [Luke] describes are associated with table fellowship" (*The IVP New Testament Commentary Series, Luke,* Downers Grove, Ill.: InterVarsity, 1994, p. 385). This can be a helpful perspective for us in our relationship with Jesus. Think of what it is like to sit around the dinner table in conversation with family and good friends. It is in this kind of relaxed, intimate setting that God wants to commune with us.

Question 10. In personal spiritual direction, the director is often able to help the directee express his or her strong desires. But in a group Bible study, participants may find it difficult to verbalize their requests. This would be a good time to be quiet for two or three minutes. Ask participants to think privately of their request for Jesus and then be silent, noticing if they have any sense of how Jesus might respond to their requests. Individuals doing the study may also want to stop for a few minutes, reflecting on this question in silence.

Question 11. Emmaus was probably about seven miles from Jerusalem.

STUDY 8: LISTENING FOR GOD'S TRANSFORMING POWER

Question 8. We sometimes mistakenly think we need to know and understand everything about God and our relationship with him. In this situation, Jesus healed someone who did not even know his name!

Question 9. Be sure to respect the privacy of individuals in the group who may not want to share their answers to this question publicly. Encourage people to share in general if they feel uncomfortable sharing the specifics of their situations.

Question 10. In John 9:1-7, we read about the disciples' asking Jesus if sin had caused a man to be born blind. Jesus stated clearly that neither the man nor his parents sinned, "but this happened so that the work of God might be displayed in his life" (verse 3). The fact that Jesus related to the blind man and the paralyzed man differently underscores our own need to relate to people as unique individuals. God's work in our lives is perfectly suited to our needs, and God accomplishes his purposes through each of us in unique ways.

RECOMMENDED READING

Learning the art of spiritual listening is a lifelong experience. The following books have been helpful to me in my own spiritual journey as well as in my ministry of spiritual direction.

Books About Spiritual Direction

Bakke, Jeannette A. *Holy Invitations.* Grand Rapids: Baker, 2000. This is a comprehensive description of the many dimensions of the spiritual direction relationship.

Benner, David G. *Sacred Companions.* Downers Grove, Ill.: InterVarsity, 2002. This is an excellent introduction to spiritual direction with an emphasis on spiritual friendships as well as more intentional spiritual direction relationships.

Guenther, Margaret. *Holy Listening.* Cambridge, Mass.: Cowley, 1992. In this book the author describes the spiritual director as a "midwife for the soul." She includes one section that specifically addresses the issues of women and spiritual direction.

Books About Prayer, Lectio Divina, Discernment, and Spiritual Formation

Bakken, Kenneth L. *The Journey into God.* Minneapolis: Augsburg, 2000. In this book the author describes the many facets of Christian healing and the faith journey.

Foster, Richard. *Prayer.* San Francisco: HarperSanFrancisco, 2002. In this classic book the author describes twenty-one different ways to pray.

Green, Thomas H. *Weeds Among the Wheat.* Notre Dame, Ind.: Ave Maria Press, 1984. Another classic, this book is about discernment, which the author describes as the place where "prayer and action meet."

Hall, Thelma. *Too Deep for Words.* Mahwah, N.J.: Paulist Press, 1988. This is an excellent description of lectio divina as a prayer form and includes five hundred Scripture texts for prayer.

Keating, Thomas. *Invitation to Love.* New York: Continuum, 1994. This book, and others by Keating, describes Centering Prayer in practical, spiritual language.

Linn, Dennis, Sheila Fabricant Linn, and Matthew Linn. *Healing the Purpose of Your Life.* Mahwah, N.J.: Paulist Press, 1999. The Linns, in their deceptively simple-looking book, present deep, thoughtful meditations with helpful suggestions for meaningful growth toward God. This is just one of several helpful books by the Linns.

Mulholland, M. Robert. *Shaped by the Word.* Nashville: The Upper Room, 1985. Dr. Mulholland looks at ways to read the Bible for transformation rather than just for information. Another good book by the same author is *Invitation to a Journey* (Downers Grove, Ill.: InterVarsity, 1993).

Nouwen, Henri. *The Return of the Prodigal Son.* New York: Doubleday, 1994. Nouwen is one of my favorite authors. He draws his readers to God with his authentic scriptural observations about life. Another excellent book by the same author is *Making All Things New* (San Francisco: HarperSanFrancisco, 1998).

Palmer, Parker J. *Let Your Life Speak.* Hoboken, N.J.: John Wiley & Sons, 1999. This is a small book with a wealth of wisdom about how to listen to your own heart in discerning God's will for you.

Peterson, Eugene H. *The Contemplative Pastor.* Grand Rapids: Eerdmans, 2002. I do not think this book is just for pastors. The author discusses the value of a contemplative lifestyle for all of us.

Rohr, Richard. *Everything Belongs.* New York: Crossroad, 2003. Author Richard Rohr describes how to live life in a contemplative way, knowing that every breath we take belongs to God.

Silf, Margaret. *Inner Compass.* Chicago: Loyola Press, 1999. This book is full of meditative suggestions for drawing closer to God and seeing the work of the Spirit in daily life.

FOR FURTHER STUDY

If you enjoyed this Fisherman Resource, you might want to explore our full line of Fisherman Resources and Bible Studyguides. The following books offer time-tested Fisherman inductive Bible studies for individuals or groups.

FISHERMAN RESOURCES

The Art of Spiritual Listening: Responding to God's Voice Amid the Noise of Life by Alice Fryling

Balm in Gilead by Dudley Delffs

The Essential Bible Guide by Whitney T. Kuniholm

Questions from the God Who Needs No Answers: What Is He Really Asking of You? by Carolyn and Craig Williford

Reckless Faith: Living Passionately as Imperfect Christians by Jo Kadlecek

Soul Strength: Spiritual Courage for the Battles of Life by Pam Lau

FISHERMAN BIBLE STUDYGUIDES

Topical Studies

Angels by Vinita Hampton Wright

Becoming Women of Purpose by Ruth Haley Barton

Building Your House on the Lord: A Firm Foundation for Family Life (Revised Edition) by Steve and Dee Brestin

Discipleship: The Growing Christian's Lifestyle by James and Martha Reapsome

Doing Justice, Showing Mercy: Christian Action in Today's World by Vinita Hampton Wright

Encouraging Others: Biblical Models for Caring by Lin Johnson

The End Times: Discovering What the Bible Says by E. Michael Rusten

Examining the Claims of Jesus by Dee Brestin

Friendship: Portraits in God's Family Album by Steve and Dee Brestin

The Fruit of the Spirit: Growing in Christian Character by Stuart Briscoe

Great Doctrines of the Bible by Stephen Board

Great Passages of the Bible by Carol Plueddemann

Great Prayers of the Bible by Carol Plueddemann

Growing Through Life's Challenges by James and Martha Reapsome

Guidance & God's Will by Tom and Joan Stark

Heart Renewal: Finding Spiritual Refreshment by Ruth Goring

Higher Ground: Steps Toward Christian Maturity by Steve and Dee Brestin

Images of Redemption: God's Unfolding Plan Through the Bible by Ruth E. Van Reken

Integrity: Character from the Inside Out by Ted W. Engstrom and Robert C. Larson

Lifestyle Priorities by John White

Marriage: Learning from Couples in Scripture by R. Paul and Gail Stevens

Miracles by Robbie Castleman

One Body, One Spirit: Building Relationships in the Church by Dale and Sandy Larsen

The Parables of Jesus by Gladys Hunt

Parenting with Purpose and Grace by Alice Fryling

Prayer: Discovering What Scripture Says by Timothy Jones and Jill Zook-Jones

The Prophets: God's Truth Tellers by Vinita Hampton Wright

Proverbs and Parables: God's Wisdom for Living by Dee Brestin

Satisfying Work: Christian Living from Nine to Five by R. Paul Stevens and Gerry Schoberg

Senior Saints: Growing Older in God's Family by James and Martha Reapsome

The Sermon on the Mount: The God Who Understands Me by Gladys M. Hunt

Speaking Wisely: Exploring the Power of Words by Poppy Smith

Spiritual Disciplines: The Tasks of a Joyful Life by Larry Sibley

Spiritual Gifts by Karen Dockrey

Spiritual Hunger: Filling Your Deepest Longings by Jim and Carol Plueddemann

A Spiritual Legacy: Faith for the Next Generation by Chuck and Winnie Christensen

Spiritual Warfare by A. Scott Moreau

The Ten Commandments: God's Rules for Living by Stuart Briscoe

Ultimate Hope for Changing Times by Dale and Sandy Larsen

When Faith Is All You Have: A Study of Hebrews 11 by Ruth E. Van Reken

Where Your Treasure Is: What the Bible Says About Money by James and Martha Reapsome

Who Is God? by David P. Seemuth

Who Is Jesus? In His Own Words by Ruth E. Van Reken

Who Is the Holy Spirit? by Barbara H. Knuckles and Ruth E. Van Reken

Wisdom for Today's Woman: Insights from Esther by Poppy Smith

Witnesses to All the World: God's Heart for the Nations by Jim and Carol Plueddemann

Women at Midlife: Embracing the Challenges by Jeanie Miley

Worship: Discovering What Scripture Says by Larry Sibley

Bible Book Studies

Genesis: Walking with God by Margaret Fromer and Sharrel Keyes

Exodus: God Our Deliverer by Dale and Sandy Larsen

Ruth: Relationships That Bring Life by Ruth Haley Barton

Ezra and Nehemiah: A Time to Rebuild by James Reapsome

(For Esther, see Topical Studies, *Wisdom for Today's Woman*)

Job: Trusting Through Trials by Ron Klug

Psalms: A Guide to Prayer and Praise by Ron Klug

Proverbs: Wisdom That Works by Vinita Hampton Wright

Ecclesiastes: A Time for Everything by Stephen Board

Song of Songs: A Dialogue of Intimacy by James Reapsome

Jeremiah: The Man and His Message by James Reapsome

Jonah, Habakkuk, and Malachi: Living Responsibly by Margaret Fromer
 and Sharrel Keyes

Matthew: People of the Kingdom by Larry Sibley

Mark: God in Action by Chuck and Winnie Christensen

Luke: Following Jesus by Sharrel Keyes

John: The Living Word by Whitney Kuniholm

Acts 1–12: God Moves in the Early Church by Chuck and Winnie
 Christensen

Acts 13–28, see *Paul* under Character Studies

Romans: The Christian Story by James Reapsome

1 Corinthians: Problems and Solutions in a Growing Church by Charles
 and Ann Hummel

Strengthened to Serve: 2 Corinthians by Jim and Carol Plueddemann

Galatians, Titus, and Philemon: Freedom in Christ by Whitney Kuniholm

Ephesians: Living in God's Household by Robert Baylis

Philippians: God's Guide to Joy by Ron Klug

Colossians: Focus on Christ by Luci Shaw

Letters to the Thessalonians by Margaret Fromer and Sharrel Keyes

Letters to Timothy: Discipleship in Action by Margaret Fromer and Sharrel
 Keyes

Hebrews: Foundations for Faith by Gladys Hunt

James: Faith in Action by Chuck and Winnie Christensen

1 and 2 Peter, Jude: Called for a Purpose by Steve and Dee Brestin
1, 2, 3 John: How Should a Christian Live? by Dee Brestin
Revelation: The Lamb Who Is the Lion by Gladys Hunt

Bible Character Studies

Abraham: Model of Faith by James Reapsome
David: Man After God's Own Heart by Robbie Castleman
Elijah: Obedience in a Threatening World by Robbie Castleman
Great People of the Bible by Carol Plueddemann
King David: Trusting God for a Lifetime by Robbie Castleman
Men Like Us: Ordinary Men, Extraordinary God by Paul Heidebrecht
    and Ted Scheuermann
Moses: Encountering God by Greg Asimakoupoulos
Paul: Thirteenth Apostle (Acts 13–28) by Chuck and Winnie Christensen
Women Like Us: Wisdom for Today's Issues by Ruth Haley Barton
Women Who Achieved for God by Winnie Christensen
Women Who Believed God by Winnie Christensen

ABOUT THE AUTHOR

ALICE FRYLING is a spiritual director, freelance writer, and conference speaker. She frequently speaks to student groups and women's conferences, gives seminars on relationship topics, and counsels engaged and married couples with her husband, Bob. Alice is the author of numerous books, including *A Handbook for Engaged Couples, A Handbook for Married Couples, Disciplemakers' Handbook, Too Busy?* and the Fisherman Bible Studyguide *Parenting with Purpose and Grace.* The Frylings have two married daughters and two grandsons.

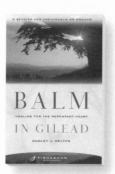
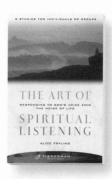

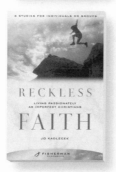